The Game Changed

POETS ON POETRY

Annie Finch and Marilyn Hacker, General Editors
Donald Hall, Founding Editor

New titles

Kazim Ali, *Orange Alert*
Martín Espada, *The Lover of a Subversive Is Also a Subversive*
Marilyn Hacker, *Unauthorized Voices*
Andrew Hudgins, *Diary of a Poem*
Lawrence Joseph, *The Game Changed*
David Mason, *Two Minds of a Western Poet*
Cole Swensen, *Noise That Stays Noise*

Recently published

Meena Alexander, *Poetics of Dislocation*
Annie Finch, *The Body of Poetry*
Sandra M. Gilbert, *On Burning Ground: Thirty Years of Thinking About Poetry*
Grace Schulman, *First Loves and Other Adventures*
Reginald Shepherd, *Orpheus in the Bronx*
Reginald Shepherd, *A Martian Muse: Further Essays on Identity, Politics, and the Freedom of Poetry*

Also available, collections by

Elizabeth Alexander, A. R. Ammons, John Ashbery, Robert Bly,
Philip Booth, Marianne Boruch, Hayden Carruth, Amy Clampitt,
Alfred Corn, Douglas Crase, Robert Creeley, Donald Davie,
Thomas M. Disch, Ed Dorn, Tess Gallagher, Dana Gioia,
Linda Gregerson, Allen Grossman, Thom Gunn, Rachel Hadas,
John Haines, Donald Hall, Joy Harjo, Robert Hayden, Edward Hirsch,
Daniel Hoffman, Jonathan Holden, John Hollander, Paul Hoover,
Andrew Hudgins, Laura (Riding) Jackson, Josephine Jacobsen,
Mark Jarman, Galway Kinnell, Kenneth Koch, John Koethe,
Yusef Komunyakaa, Maxine Kumin, Martin Lammon (editor),
Philip Larkin, David Lehman, Philip Levine, Larry Levis, John Logan,
William Logan, William Matthews, William Meredith, Jane Miller,
David Mura, Carol Muske, Alice Notley, Geoffrey O'Brien, Gregory Orr,
Alicia Suskin Ostriker, Ron Padgett, Marge Piercy, Anne Sexton,
Karl Shapiro, Charles Simic, William Stafford, Anne Stevenson,
May Swenson, James Tate, Richard Tillinghast, C. K. Williams,
Alan Williamson, Charles Wright, James Wright, John Yau, and
Stephen Yenser

Lawrence Joseph

The Game Changed

ESSAYS AND OTHER PROSE

THE UNIVERSITY OF MICHIGAN PRESS

Ann Arbor

Published in the United States of America by
The University of Michigan Press
Manufactured in the United States of America
♾ Printed on acid-free paper

2014   2013   2012   2011   4   3   2   1

A CIP catalog record for this book is available from the British Library.

Library of Congress Cataloging-in-Publication Data

Joseph, Lawrence, 1948–
     The game changed : essays and other prose / Lawrence Joseph.
        p.   cm. — (Poets on poetry series)
     ISBN 978-0-472-07161-6 (cloth : alk. paper) — ISBN 978-0-472-
05161-8 (pbk. : alk. paper) — ISBN 978-0-472-02774-3 (ebk.)
     1. Joseph, Lawrence, 1948– Knowledge—Poetry.   2. Poetry.
I. Title.
PS3560.O775G36   2011
814'.54—dc22   2011014828

For Laurence Goldstein

Acknowledgments

"The Poet and the Lawyer: The Example of Wallace Stevens" was presented as a talk at the Eleventh Annual Wallace Stevens Birthday Bash, sponsored by The Hartford Friends of Wallace Stevens, at the Hartford Public Library, on October 7, 2006.

"Michael Schmidt's *Lives of the Poets*" originally appeared in *The Nation*, December 13, 1999, under the title "New Poetics (Sans Aristotle)."

"A Note on 'That's All'" originally appeared, in slightly different form, in *Ecstatic Occasions, Expedient Forms*, edited by David Lehman (Macmillan, 1987).

"Tony Harrison and Michael Hofmann" originally appeared, in slightly different form, in *The Village Voice*, March 20, 1990, under the title "Men of Irony."

"Frederick Seidel" originally appeared, in slightly different form, in *The Nation*, September 24, 1990, under the title "War of the Worlds."

Parts of "Enzensberger's *Kiosk*" appeared, in different form, in *Jacket #4*, and in the "Preface" to *Kiosk* (The Sheep Meadow Press, 1998).

"'Our Lives Are Here': Notes from a Journal, Detroit, 1975" originally appeared, in slightly different form, in *Michigan Quarterly Review* (Spring 1986).

"John Ashbery and Adrienne Rich" originally appeared, in slightly different form, in *The Nation*, April 20, 1992, under the title "The Real Thing."

"James Schuyler's *The Morning of the Poem*" originally appeared, in slightly different form, in *Poetry East* (Fall 1992).

"Word Made Flesh" originally appeared, in different form, in *Communities: Contemporary Writers Reveal the Bible in Their Lives*, edited by David Rosenberg (Archer Books, 1996), under the title "Jeremiah and Corinthians."

The first two parts of "A Few Reflections on Poetry and Language" originally appeared, in different form, in "Theories of Poetry, Theories of Law," *Vanderbilt Law Review* (Volume 46, 1993).

"Hayden Carruth" originally appeared, in slightly different form, in *The Kenyon Review* (Winter 1994), under the title "Journeys to Love."

"Marilyn Hacker" originally appeared, in slightly different form, in *Voice Literary Supplement,* February 1995, under the title "A Formal Life: Marilyn Hacker's Deep Structure."

"Aspects of Weldon Kees" originally appeared in *Verse* (Summer 1997), under the title "Aspects of Kees."

"Smokey Robinson's High Tenor Voice" originally appeared in *Michigan Quarterly Review* (Fall 2000).

"Joyce Carol Oates's *Blonde*" originally appeared in *The Nation,* May 8, 2000, under the title "Where Are You Going, Where Have You Been?"

"Marie Ponsot" originally appeared, in slightly different form, in *Commonweal,* December 18, 2009, under the title "Between Silence & Sound."

"Conversation with Charles Bernstein" is transcribed, in slightly different form, from *A New Close Listening and Reading and Conversation with Lawrence Joseph,* PennSound, July 7, 2008, http://www.writing.upenn.edu/pennsound/daily/200807.php.

"Working Rules for *Lawyerland*" originally appeared in *Columbia Law Review* (Volume 101, 2001).

"Being in the Language of Poetry, Being in the Language of Law" was presented as the Colin Ruagh Thomas O'Fallon Memorial Lecture, University of Oregon Humanities Center, April 16, 2009, and published, in different form, in *Oregon Law Review* (Volume 88, 2010).

The selections in the "Poets on Poets and Poetry" sections are also included in "Notions of Poetry and Narration," *Cincinnati Law Review* (Volume 77, 2009).

My thanks to Andrew Simons, William Manz, and, especially, Marilyn Hacker and Peter Oresick.

Contents

Poets on Poets and Poetry

The Poet and the Lawyer: The Example of
Wallace Stevens   3

Michael Schmidt's *Lives of the Poets*   10

A Note on "That's All"   18

Tony Harrison and Michael Hofmann   21

Frederick Seidel   26

Enzensberger's *Kiosk*   33

"Our Lives Are Here": Notes from a Journal,
Detroit, 1975   42

John Ashbery and Adrienne Rich   50

Poets on Poets and Poetry

James Schuyler's *The Morning of the Poem*   59

Word Made Flesh   68

A Few Reflections on Poetry and Language   78

Hayden Carruth   89

Marilyn Hacker   95

Aspects of Weldon Kees   99

Smokey Robinson's High Tenor Voice   104

Joyce Carol Oates's *Blonde*   106

Poets on Poets and Poetry

Marie Ponsot   115

Conversation with Charles Bernstein   120

Working Rules for *Lawyerland*   129

The Game Changed   133

Being in the Language of Poetry, Being in the Language
of Law   140

Poets on Poets and Poetry

Adrienne Rich, in *Poetry & Commitment: An Essay*: "Poetries are no more pure and simple than human histories are pure and simple."

Thomas Merton, in his 1967 essay "Day of a Stranger": "There is a mental ecology, too, in living balance of spirits in this corner of the woods. There is room here for many songs. Vallejo for instance. Or Rilke, or René Char, Montale, Zukofsky, Ungaretti, Edwin Muir, Quasimodo or some Greeks. Or the dry, disconcerting voice of Nicanor Parra. Here is the reassuring companionship of many silent Tzu's and Fu's; King Tzu, Lao Tzu, Meng Tzu, Tu Fu. And Nui Neng. And Chao-Chu. And the drawings of Sengai. And a big graceful scroll from Suzuki. Here also is a Syrian hermit called Philoxenus. And an Algerian cenobite called Camus. Here is heard the clanging prose of Tertullian. . . . Here the voluble dissonances of Auden, with the golden sounds of John of Salisbury. Here is the deep vegetation of that more ancient forest in which the angry Isaias and Jeremias sing. Here are voices from Angela of Foligno to Flannery O'Connor, Theresa of Avila, Juliana of Norwich. . . . It is good to choose the voices that will be heard in these woods, but they also choose themselves, and send themselves to be present in this silence. In any case there is no lack of voices."

The Poet and the Lawyer

The Example of Wallace Stevens

I

"The slight tobaccoy odor of autumn"—Wallace Stevens begins his introduction to Williams Carlos Williams's 1934 *Collected Poems*—"is perceptible in these pages. Williams is past fifty."

Autumn this evening is perceptible in Hartford. Wallace Stevens was born 127 years ago this past Monday . . .

I knew I would write poetry forty years ago, during the autumn of 1966, my first semester as an undergraduate at the University of Michigan. I had elected an upper level "Introduction to Poetry" course and the class was assigned "The Emperor of Ice Cream" by Wallace Stevens. I was also taking an upper level course in Latin, which concentrated on Book VIII of Virgil's *Aeneid*. In the evenings, in the University's Main Library, I would work through Virgil, and then through the poems assigned in "Introduction to Poetry." I usually had some sense of a poem's meanings—poems by Milton and Donne, Spenser and Eliot, Coleridge and Dickinson, Pound, Frost, Moore, Hopkins. But "The Emperor of Ice Cream"—I had no idea what it was about, which both frustrated and intrigued me. After the professor took us through it, explaining its multiple meanings as best he could, I felt that this was the highest form of expression, and that I wanted to emulate it. I wanted to create this kind of art—to create poems that would have the same effect on a reader that Wallace Stevens's poem had on me.

Professor Coles would provide literary and biographical information about each poet. He told the class that for most of his life Stevens had been a bond lawyer with the Hartford Accident

3

and Indemnity Company in Hartford. I distinctly remember him saying this. I was raised to be a lawyer. My grandparents were Lebanese and Syrian Catholics who emigrated to Detroit before World War I. My mother and father were born in Detroit after the war ended. My grandparents on both sides were grocers. Each spoke and read and wrote Arabic—they also learned to speak English quickly and proficiently—but could neither read nor write English. My parents, my aunts and my uncles, all born in Detroit, were educated in Catholic grade and high schools. My father and his brother inherited their father's grocery store, which became a grocery party-liquor store. It was located in Detroit's most violent neighborhood during the nineteen-fifties and sixties. The only member of the family of my parents' generation who did not enter into that declining business of city-family-owned grocery stores was my mother's younger and only brother, who, after being in a Catholic seminary for his college years (the first of his generation to have gone to college), left the seminary and attended law school at the University of Detroit. Our uncle was held up to me and my older brother by both my father and mother as an example. Both my brother and I became lawyers.

I began law school in 1973, at Michigan again, after two years of postgraduate studies in English Language and Literature at Magdalene College, the University of Cambridge. I had been writing poetry since that autumn of 1966 and have continued to write it to this day. Since that autumn forty years ago, whenever I've thought of Wallace Stevens, I've thought of him both as a poet and as a lawyer.

II

In 1900, after three years at Harvard—his undeniable talent for writing poetry recognized by his peers and his professors—Wallace Stevens moved to New York City, where, with the intention of devoting his life to writing poetry, he worked the overnight shift as a journalist for the *New York Tribune*. After a year as a journalist, Stevens took the advice of his father, who was a lawyer, and followed his father and his two brothers to law school, entering New York Law School, in downtown Manhattan, in the fall of 1901. Three years later, in 1904, he was admitted to the New York Bar. He then practiced, on and off, for four years with a number of private firms. In 1908, he took a job with the American Bonding Company, handled claims made on the company's surety bonds. He left American Bonding in 1913 for the Equitable Surety Company, having acquired a specialty in surety bonds. When, three years later, Equitable unexpectedly failed, Stevens took a position with the Hartford Accident and Indemnity Company in Hartford, where he not only covered surety claims, but also oversaw the legal affairs of Hartford's expanding bond claims department. By 1918, Hartford had established a separate surety bond department, which Stevens headed for the rest of his life. In 1934, he was promoted to vice president, becoming one of four vice presidents of one of the major insurance companies in the United States.

In 1983, Random House published Peter Brazeau's *Parts of a World: Wallace Stevens Remembered, An Oral Biography*. After law school and a two-year judicial clerkship in Detroit with a justice of the Michigan Supreme Court, and then three years as a member of the University of Detroit School of Law faculty, I was—at the time that the Brazeau book came out—practicing law in New York City. That year, my first book of poems, *Shouting at No One*, was published.

Until Brazeau's book, poets and critics (as well as the continuously growing readership of Stevens's poetry) thought generally of Stevens as a poet who also underwrote insurance. Brazeau's interviews with Stevens's former colleagues at the Hartford made clear what Professor Coles had said, that Stevens was a lawyer. The most succinct and accurate description of Stevens's law practice that I know of, is found in Stanford law professor Thomas C. Grey's indispensable book on Stevens, *The Wallace Stevens Case: Law and the Practice of Poetry*:

> On a typical working day, Stevens came to his office around nine, read his mail, then turned to the stack of files of claims requiring review, and worked on them systematically through the day. He was renowned both for his steady diligence at work ("the grindingest guy . . . in executive row") and for his meticulous attention to detail; he left a clear desk at the end

of each day, and did not take work home. Stevens stayed in his office, cherishing his solitude as he ground through his files. A number of colleagues recall him reacting with annoyance when interrupted, even for a business purpose, or continuing to work head down, for long minutes as they silently waited. No office politician, he was often famously undiplomatic, with superiors as well as subordinates, peers, outside agents, and other sources of company business. . . .

A surety bond is a promise by the insurer to pay a legal obligation of an insured; its purpose is to assure third parties who are at risk of loss if the insured becomes insolvent. To take the most common example, a builder might have to post a performance surety bond in order to get a construction job; the bond means that if the builder doesn't finish the job or botches it, the insurance company as surety will pay the resulting damages to the other party, even if the builder has gone broke in the meantime. . . .

As Stevens reviewed surety claims, he was making both legal and business judgments. On the legal side, he had to decide whether the claim was valid. Did the insured builder, for example, breach its contract? The insurance company could assert any defense available to the builder (for example, breach of a condition on the part of the claimant); deciding whether such a defense existed required close investigation of the facts and review of the original contract. . . .

When he judged a claim to be valid, there remained, in contractor bond cases, the decision whether to pay off the bond or attempt to finish the work contracted for. Here is where Stevens achieved his greatest reputation; he was "a very imaginative claims man" . . . . The decision required evaluating which contracts could still be performed for less than the damages payable to the other party, and thus at a profit to the company. Good judgment on such matters required being "highly practical, realistic" . . . . It was in connection with this ability of Stevens's that colleagues came to judge him "the dean of surety claims men in the whole country."

III

"Poetry and surety claims aren't as unlikely a combination as they may seem," Stevens once remarked. He did not have, he said, a separate mind for legal work and another for writing poetry; he did each with his whole mind. The Stevens who specialized in surety law possessed enormous capacities of concentration and focus. He was expert at the various legal languages that came into play in the practice of surety law. He could absorb extraordinarily complex sets of facts, while moving them in his mind through the complex languages of the applicable substantive law. He was diligent and disciplined. He was tough-minded. He was a note-taker (as most lawyers are) and did his own research (which he liked to do). He preferred to work alone. He was highly demanding on himself. His work required that he read almost all the time. The Stevens who wrote poems also worked in his mind, composing while he walked to and from work, after dinner, before sleep. The making of a poem was, for him, a solitary act of the mind, which he wholly engaged in. He was always jotting down notes when thoughts of poems came to mind, often during his workday. His appetite for reading was wide-ranging. "I have been making notes on the subject in the form of short poems during the past winter," he wrote in reference to what became the poem "The Man with the Blue Guitar." "Poetry is, of all others," he noted in his commonplace book, "the most daring form of research." "Poetry," he noted in his *Adagia*, "is the scholar's art."

There was nothing perfunctory, Stevens once said, about the handling of a bond claim. Each case had its own facts and issues, its own legal language, each case had its own requirements and demands. There was nothing perfunctory, either, Stevens said, about writing a poem. Each poem was different, with its own issues, its own language. "Poetry," Stevens once told a fellow worker, "is what you feel, and what you sense, and how you say it." "Poetry," Stevens wrote, "seeks out the relation of men to facts." Poetry, he said during World War II, presses back against the "pressures" of factual reality. Reviewing *The Man with the Blue Guitar* for the *Partisan Review* in 1938, Delmore Schwartz observed that, from the beginning, Stevens's poetry was "absorbed in 'response' to various facts," absorbed, Schwartz added, "to such an extent, that the facts can scarcely get into the poems at all. By thus placing facts within the poem, the responses to the facts gain immeasurable strength and relevance. We may compare

Stevens"—Schwartz went on—"to William Carlos Williams, whom Stevens admires, and who may be said to represent the other extreme, a poet whose whole effort is to get the facts into his poem with the greatest exactitude and to keep everything else out." In Stevens's poems there are no specific scenes, nor times, nor actions, "but only the mind moving among its meanings and replying to situations which are referred to, but not contained in, the poems themselves. The poems, because of the extent of the poet's awareness, are located in the middle of everything which concerns us."

IV

In a 1945 letter, Stevens wrote: "Moreover, in the world of actuality . . . one is always living a little out of it. There is a precious sentence in Henry James, for whom everyday life was not much more than the mere business of living, but, all the same, he separated himself from it. The sentence is . . . 'To live in the world of creation—to get into it and stay in it—to frequent it and haunt it—to think intensely and fruitfully—to woo combinations and inspirations into being by a depth and continuity of attention and meditation—this is the only thing.'" I use this quotation as the epigraph of my book of poems, *Into It*.

Combinations of fact and thought, of feeling and meaning, pressured into the depth and intensity of composed language; these lines are from Stevens's poem "Large Red Man Reading" in *The Auroras of Autumn*:

> There were ghosts that returned to earth to hear his
> phrases,
> As he sat there reading, aloud, the great blue tabulae.
> They were those from the wilderness of stars that had
> expected more.
>
> There were those that returned to hear him read from the
> poem of life,
> Of the pans above the stove, the pots on the table, the tulips
> among them.
> They were those that would have wept to step barefoot into
> reality

They would have wept and then been happy, have shivered
    in the frost
And cried out to feel it again, have run fingers over leaves
And against the most coiled thorn, have seized on what was
    ugly

And laughed, as he sat there reading, from out of the
    purple tabulae,
The outlines of being and its expressions, the syllables of its
    law:
Poesis, poesis, the literal characters, the vatic lines . . .

And, these lines from Stevens's poem "Of Modern Poetry," in
Parts of a World:

The poem of the mind in the act of finding
What will suffice. It has not always had
To find: the scene was set; it repeated what
Was in the script.
          Then the theatre was changed
To something else. Its past was a souvenir . . .

                    . . . It must
Be the finding of a satisfaction, and may
Be of a man skating, a woman dancing, a woman
Combing. The poem of the act of the mind.

V

And, so, we celebrate him this evening, in this city where he
lived and worked for forty years, writing a body of poems unparalleled in American literature. So, on this autumn evening
in Hartford, we celebrate the tremendous satisfaction that this
large red man's readings have given us—the poems of the acts of
the mind both of the poet and the lawyer, the vitally compounded
and combined acts of his *poesis*, the syllables of its law.

    Happy birthday, Mr. Stevens.

Michael Schmidt's *Lives of the Poets*

The book equivalent of a poetsbiography.com? How about, instead, more than sixty essay-like stories, with titles like "'Not as I
suld, I wrait, but as I couth': Robert Henryson, William Dunbar,
Gavin Douglas, Stephen Hawes" and "'Arranging, deepening,
enchanting': Wallace Stevens, Marianne Moore, Elizabeth
Bishop, John Ashbery, Amy Clampitt, Sharon Olds, Mark Doty"?
A *summa poetica* that begins with a piece titled "The Match":
"While the Irish football team played the Soviet Union in 1988,
four English poets were confined in a radio studio in Dublin—
it was the Writers' Conference—to take part in a round-table
discussion. English-language poets, that is, for none of them"—
Seamus Heaney, Derek Walcott, Joseph Brodsky, Les Murray—
"accepts the sobriquet 'English.' In the chair . . . an anglophone
Mexican publisher, me."

The "me"—Michael Schmidt, born of American parents in
Mexico in 1947—is quite consciously and strategically present
in his *Lives* from the outset. Schmidt's first language was Spanish (he has translated Octavio Paz, among others), American
English his second. He attended Harvard and then Oxford,
where, in the late sixties, he began his life as a publisher and
editor, starting Carcanet Press. In 1972, he founded the poetry
magazine *PN Review,* which he also edits. Carcanet has published more than a thousand titles, mostly poetry, but challenging fiction as well, including translations from other literatures,
from every time period. In addition to his publishing and editorial work, Schmidt directs the writing school at Manchester
Metropolitan University. In his spare time, he's managed to
publish poetry, fiction, essays, reviews, and other critical writing.

"A poet grows, poetry grows. The growth of poetry is the
story of poems, where they come from and how they change";

for Schmidt, a poet who uses the English language is a kind of anthologist. "Figuratively speaking, John Gower and Geoffrey Chaucer lined up the French poems and classical stories they were going to transpose into English; they marked passages to expand or excise. From secondary sources (in memory, or on parchment) they culled images, passages, facts, to slot into their new context. Then began the process of making those resources reconfigure for *their* poem." Where, Schmidt asks, did this English poetic medium come from? What makes it cohere? One thing: Its history isn't linear. "There's no straight line, it's all zigzags . . . Poems swim free of their age and live in ours."

Yet, says Schmidt, a poem never "swims entirely free of its medium," which is "language used in the particular ways that are poetry." For three-quarters of a millennium, English poetry has been "gathering into standard forms." It then began to diversify into dialects that became languages of their own. In the early part of the century, Ezra Pound (born in Hailey, Idaho, in 1885) declared that English was a foreign language. But at the end of the twentieth century—the round-table discussion during the soccer match in Dublin is early evidence of it—there is, Schmidt argues, a common "English," expressed in different ways and to individual ends. The story of this language—whose subjects arise out of religious belief and doubt; out of history, politics, war, and economics; out of anxiety, sexual desire, or frustration; out of love and hate—affirms continuity. Its continuity is not only geographical but historical, "analogies and real connections between Eavan Boland and Alfred, Lord Tennyson, Allen Ginsberg and William Blake, John Ashbery and Thomas Lovell Beddoes, Thom Gunn and Ben Jonson, Elizabeth Bishop and Alexander Pope." It is, Schmidt maintains, a story that thrives when language itself is interrogated, "from the moment John Gower challenged himself, 'Why *not* write in English?'" to Wordsworth calling for a "language closer to speech" to Adrienne Rich asking, "Why write in the forms that a tradition hostile to me and my kind prescribes?"

Interrogate poetry in the English language from its beginnings in the fourteenth century to the time that he's writing: That's Schmidt's project. So why not write it in a language that is close to speech? Why not invent a form in which to write it? Why not write a personal perspective into the story? Not the perspective of a linguist, a prosodist, a historian, a philosopher, a critic, or a poet; instead, that of a publisher whose specialty is the making of books? What does a publisher know about poetry? Well, to begin with, he knows how to read it. After all, he is the first one to read almost every poem that travels beyond the poet's circle of charmed friends, the one who changes and abridges, cuts and adds, whose responsibility is *getting it right*. He is, as a reader, bound, of course, to make errors of emphasis, of fact, of commission and omission. But he's also at liberty to evolve his own method of setting a poem free. To do that, says Schmidt, you have to know how to *hear* a poem fully. "If in a twentieth-century poem about social and psychological disruption a sudden line of eighteenth-century construction irrupts, the reader who is not alert to the irony in diction and cadence is not alert to the poem. A texture of tones and ironies, or a texture of voices such as we get in John Ashbery, or elegiac strategies in Philip Larkin, or Eastern forms in Elizabeth Daryush and Judith Wright, or prose transpositions in Marianne Moore and (differently) in Patricia Beer: anyone aspiring to be the greatest reader in the world needs to hear in a poem read aloud or on the page what it is made from." The fascinating story of poetic growth isn't factual biography or the rehashing of political or literary fashion. It is a deeper story, revealed through the reading of—the listening to—the way in which language is employed in a poem.

A life of poetry in the English language—until the twentieth century, Schmidt's approach to his subject is chronological. Poets, for the most part, are grouped together. For example, under the title "Entr'acte," we have Charles of Orleans, Thomas Hoccleave, John Lydgate, and Juliana Berners. A few—John Gower, Geoffrey Chaucer, "Anon," William Caxton (a fellow publisher), John Skelton, Edmund Spenser, Thomas Campion, William Blake—enjoy their own chapters. Only Dr. Johnson— his *Lives of the English Poets* is for Schmidt an obvious formal influence (but not as much an influence as Ford Madox Ford's *The March of Literature*)—has a chapter named after him. Who gets how much space and what kind of attention is a matter of personal decision; Schmidt does not pretend to neutrality. He knows that language—his own included—no matter how it is expressed, contains the speech of a real person. Schmidt's language isn't, however, simply subjective. It is more accurately a language that engages its subject—the probing of the life of the poem. Engagement propels the entire book. From the get-go, Schmidt exudes intensity. Tones of voice change—sometimes he is openly conversational, other times excessively dense, sometimes downright nasty, other times eloquently generous. Countless sentences pop at you aphoristically ("Jonson suffers one irremediable disability: Shakespeare"). Observations by poets about poets are generously quoted, becoming, compositionally, not only a part of the talk but of the story as well ("'Byron knew and regretted the colossal vulgarity, which he shrouded by a cloak of aloof grandeur,' Robert Graves suggests. 'It was a studious vulgarity: cosmetics and curl papers tended his elegant beauty; an ingenious, though synthetic, verse technique smoothed his cynical Spenserian stanzas'"). At times, the language is maddeningly cursory; other times exquisitely nuanced. Favorite poems are mentioned at times only by title; others are quoted in part or in whole. Of course, you prefer some passages to others—you prefer some poets to others—and, among those passages you prefer, some of them you prefer enormously. Other passages don't interest you much at all.

There are occasions when voice, insight, composition, and subject wondrously combine, for instance in Schmidt's exposition of Emily Dickinson (we're on page 474 by now), after he's mentioned Thomas Wentworth Higginson, the editor of *The Atlantic Monthly*, with whom Dickinson corresponded:

> His advice was not helpful: she must make the poems more regular, she must punctuate them more conventionally. She did not comply; seeing her poems tidied up upset her: they lost expressiveness and definition. Ironically, his advice made her more resolute in her originality.

Suddenly, Schmidt's voice shifts. It is, he says, hard to define Dickinson's originality:

> I first experienced it when Robert Frost came to my school. In a lecture he called "The Pan-Handle of Poetry," he recited eight lines of verse.

> The heart asks pleasure first,
> And then, excuse from pain;
> And then, those little anodynes
> That deaden suffering;
>
> And then, to go to sleep;
> And then, if it should be
> The will of its Inquisitor
> The liberty to die.

I was fourteen at the time and had always found her mawkish in textbooks. . . . After Frost's recitation in that slow dismissive voice of his, I knew the poem word-perfect and have never forgotten it.

Schmidt goes on:

> But it was not *her* poem, and it was not word-perfect. This was the version Mabel Loomis Todd published, shaking out the loose straw of the poet's dashes, taking down her capital letters and, where a word seemed ominously suspended by a definite article, assigning it by a possessive pronoun. . . . The version Frost should have recited (though, an old man, he stuck with the one he had known for years) was this one: different diction, punctuation, rhythm:
>
>> The Heart asks Pleasure—first—
>> And then—Excuse from Pain—
>> And then—those little Anodynes
>> That deaden suffering—
>>
>> And then—to go to sleep—
>> And then—if it should be
>> The will of the Inquisitor
>> The privilege to die—

"Here," he says, "is the originality,"

> unmuffled after eight decades of propriety, an irregularity that answers to the darting, tentative process of the poet's sight and feeling, the rapid transformations that follow an unfolding argument or feeling. Dickinson's poetry is the drama of *process*; "The Heart asks Pleasure" is nothing less than an essential autobiography.

As he approaches the present, Schmidt pauses to catch his breath—and to modify his strategy. Chronology is abandoned; "big lights" of the first half of the century are used to define "orbits" into which other poets are drawn. (Not all the poets in orbit are treated entirely with favor.) From the fourteenth to the twentieth century—two-thirds of the book—130 poets are mentioned; from the twenties to the present, about two hundred. How many serious poets have there been in the English language since the twenties? Thirty thousand?—each, of course, convinced that at least one or two of his or her poems are immortal, and that he or she should be immortalized in an omnibus *Lives of the Poets.* Schmidt realizes how high-risk the fame game is, proffering numerous caveats: "Had this account been written in 1798, would I have felt compelled to include Sir John Denham, John Pomfret, George Stepney, Richard Duke, Samuel Garth, John Hughes, Elijah Fenton, Gilbert West, David Mallet, and thirty or so others?"

Now that he's in the present, Schmidt also puts his biases up front. He will continue to place a high value on the work of poets that he thinks may influence the future growth of the art and the language. But, as poetry in the English language faces a future of unparalleled diversity and volatile new technology, he will also look to poetry "sufficiently capacious to accommodate a variety of needs and responses," insisting on "plurality as against faction and canonical closure." Ethnicity, gender, and gender preference will be acknowledged if they open poetic space—a space now occupied by an "English" language as different and yet similar in sound as the poems of Edwin Morgan, Richard Wilbur, Sujata Bhatt, and Edward Kamau Brathwaite. The foundation of Schmidt's aesthetic is what he refers to as a poetry of "radical imagination," by which he means poetry that refines and defines the art, paying tribute to tradition by innovation and extension, distrusting the orthodoxies of the age. His bearings—though he loves Thomas Hardy and Frost—are modernist. It is a modernism firmly rooted in the almost anachronistic belief that it's possible to find coherence in a large body of work from many different parts of the world—the modernism, for example, of Pound, Eliot, H.D., Louis Zukofsky, Basil Bunting. Postmodernist theories of incoherence Schmidt outright rejects; nor does he tolerate a New Formalism that wishes William Carlos Williams had never written a word. He is disturbed by what he sees as the prevalent mode of the day, an irony both small and strategic, a stance by which the poet, though appearing to confront the world, is in fact preserving himself from engagement, overstatement, and responsibility for what's said. The irony Schmidt prefers—that of a Hardy or a Housman—is as old as the art: the metaphysical irony with which reality confronts the human being.

Having defined his tastes, Schmidt is free to choose whom he wants to talk about and what he wants to say about them. His method is such that any agreements or disagreements with his choices (which include poets he has known and published), or with what he has to say about them, depend on whether you agree or disagree with his biases. Any reader of twentieth-century poetry will have plenty to disagree with; Schmidt, though, knows that going in. His main objective isn't the determination of which poets should be considered—it is to present a way of reading. If you disagree with him, you find yourself positing your own reasons for including or excluding a poet. One way or the other, Schmidt draws you in.

That's not to say that the gaps aren't annoying. Why isn't Tom Paulin—certainly as radically imaginative a poet and reader of poetry as anyone in England today—even mentioned? I would also think that James Merrill's poetry—who has been more experimental with form?—merits better than just two adjectives, "Augustan" and "glittering." Schmidt occasionally falls into the kind of accepted orthodoxy that he so forcefully disclaims—a good example being what he concludes about Allen Ginsberg. "The big days were in the 1950s, and his last four decades fed off the fat of the huge and unexpected pop star success of his setting out. He remained a compelling performer, even of the awful later poems. . . . It is to his first three books that future readers will attend, *Howl and Other Poems* (1956), *Kaddish and Other Poems* (1960) and *Reality Sandwiches* (1963)." Awful later poems? Many of Ginsberg's finest poems—different in structure and syntax from his earlier work—appear in later books, *The Fall of America, White Shroud,* and *Cosmopolitan Greetings.* How would Schmidt respond to these objections? Perhaps with an emphatic shrug or perhaps with heated argument; either response is of course consistent with the range of reaction that exists throughout *Lives of the Poets*.

Which is, finally, what you take away from the book: Schmidt's insistent exploration of his subjects—the unfolding drama of feeling and sound found in the language and in the lives of those who make poems. What makes *Lives of the Poets* important—why it will be read for a long time to come—is not as much Schmidt's argument as his form. "It is an act of folly, I now know, to undertake so large a task as this," Schmidt admits at the end of his story. But, as one of his "big lights," Wallace Stevens, wrote in 1938: "After all, the fury of poetry always comes from the presence of a madman or two." Isn't it, after all, deep within the fury of Schmidt's story where, finally, we find the pulse, the Heart asking Pleasure—nothing less than the essential autobiography—of the common tribe.

A Note on "That's All"

That's All

I work and I remember. I conceive
a river of cracked hands above Manhattan.

No spirit leaped with me in the womb.
No prophet explains why Korean women

thread Atomic Machinery's machines
behind massive, empty criminal tombs.

Why do I make my fire my heart's blood,
two or three ideas thought through

to their conclusions, make my air
dirty the rain around towers of iron,

a brown moon, the whole world?
My power becomes my sorrow.

Truth? My lies are sometimes true.
Firsthand, I now see the God

whose witness is revealed in tongues
before the Exchange on Broad Street

and the transfer of 2,675,000,000 dollars
by tender offer are acts of the mind,

and the calculated truths of First
National City Bank. Too often

I think about third cousins in the Shouf.
I also often think about the fact that

in 1926, after Céline visited
the Ford Rouge foundry and wrote

his treatise on the use of physically
inferior production line workers,

an officially categorized "displaced person"
tied a handkerchief around his face

to breathe the smells and the heat
in a manner so as not to destroy

his lungs and brain for four years
until he was laid off. I don't

mediate on hope and despair.
I don't deny the court that rules

my race is Jewish or Abyssinian.
In good times I transform myself

into the sun's great weight, in bad times
I make myself like smoke on flat wastes.

I don't know why I choose who I am:
I work and I remember, that's all.

ॐ

"That's All" was written in late 1982, two and a half years after
my wife Nancy and I moved to New York City from Detroit. I
wanted to write a poem that incorporated various aspects of
both cities, and of the Shouf mountains in Lebanon (from
which one of my grandfathers emigrated to Detroit, and which,
at the time, was immersed in fierce warfare). I wanted to make
emblematic images of Detroit, New York, and Lebanon: Detroit,
as an expression of labor; New York City, as an expression of fi-
nance capital; and Lebanon, as an expression of religious violence. I also wanted to create a person—the "I" of the poem—
who both reacted to and was a part of these worlds.

I needed a form that would hold the poem's multiple dimensions, but wanted it (as I want all of my poems) to achieve a
sense of control, balance, and lucidity, a classical *claritas*. I decided on a juxtapositional and somewhat disjunctive structure
expressed, stanzaically, in couplets. The form has as its imagined
base a ten-syllable line, which I vary and modulate to effectuate
the line's syntax, sound, and meanings. Weldon Kees uses this

line in many of the poems in his last collection, *Poems 1947–1954*. John Berryman also uses it in his poems in *Love & Fame* (which I consider to be his finest technical achievement).

The poem's final movement infuses the poem's "places" and the "I" within them. Its final couplet—"I don't know why I choose who I am: / I work and I remember, that's all"—is expressed with declarative restraint. Its formal lineage is classical.

Tony Harrison and
Michael Hofmann

"Deeply ironic structure" is Terry Eagleton's description of an essential quality of Tony Harrison's poetry, and he's right—not only about Harrison, but also about the poets in England who are making a permanent mark on their language. The best poets writing in England—and Tony Harrison and Michael Hofmann are among them—combine an awareness of social conflict with an acute aesthetic sense of how that conflict should be expressed in the language of English poetry. The irony that results is located within complicated cores of social and personal realities—an irony that cuts both inward and outward.

V. and Other Poems is the second book by Tony Harrison published in the United States. It appears almost three years after his *Selected Poems*, which created an enthusiastic American readership beyond the cognoscenti who had known and admired his work in its British editions. At fifty-two, Harrison is generally acknowledged as a major English poet; now working at the National Theatre, he is also a brilliant translator. His achievements are especially unusual in a country as socially divided as England. Born into England's northern working class, Harrison is a politically engaged writer in the mold of Bertolt Brecht. There has always been continuity in Harrison's work, and the poems in *V.* are no exception. In poem after poem, Harrison probes how class, language, and history intricately impose upon personal experience—always through crafty metered and rhymed structures which twist and turn around their subjects, and make the language itself an object of ironic inquiry. "Painkillers" and "Sonnets for August 1945" employ the sixteen-line Meredithian sonnet form that Harrison transformed in earlier sonnet sequences, in *The School of Eloquence* and *Continuous,* and fit comfortably within them. "Y," "Summoned by Bells," and "The Pomegrantes of Patmos" are less emotive and more satiric—Harrison twitting the twits. But three of the poems in *V. and Other Poems*—"v.," "The Heatless Art," and "The Mother of the Muses"—display an emotional intensity that is new in Harrison's work.

The title poem originally appeared in book form in 1985 from Newcastle's excellent small-trade publisher Bloodaxe Books, and comes with a quote from the London *Times* describing it as the "most publicized poem in modern history." The cause of the hoopla was a feature on "v." on British television. The Conservative MP who introduced Britain's Obscene Publications Act wanted the TV show censored because—he accused—"v." contained "a cascade of obscenities." The poem is set in the Leeds cemetery where Harrison's working-class parents are buried. During one of the poet's infrequent visits to the cemetery, he discovers the tombstones graffitied with "four-letter curses," "(mostly) FUCK!," and "Vs" spray-painted—the poet imagines—by unemployed skinhead teenage fans of the Leeds United football team (apparently a perennial loser). Harrison knows quite well that

> These Vs are all the versus of life
> from LEEDS v. DERBY, Black/White
> and (as I've known to my cost) man v. wife.
> Communist v. Fascist. Left v. Right.
>
> class v. class as bitter as before,
> the unending violence of US and THEM.
> personified in 1984
> by Coal Board MacGregor and the N.U.M.,
>
> Hindu/Sikh, soul/body, heart v. mind
> East/West, male/female, and the ground
> these fixtures are fought out on's Man, resigned
> to hope from his future what his past never found.

But when the poet finds "UNITED" graffitied on his parents' stone the ironies multiply: He is torn between his love and respect for his parents and their burial ground, his political empathy for the unemployed skinhead, and his awareness, as a poet, that he has come upon metaphors that define his entire universe. Harrison takes us through various levels of discourse (the skinhead's voice is suddenly injected into the poem, arguing with the poet, until the voice merges back into the poet's); different, conflicting, perspectives are expressed through dialogue. Finally, the dialogue becomes dialectic. The poet's resolves are classical: Realizations of love—for parents, for "my woman"—are called into relief and measured against the England that he has chosen to see.

These realizations—pronounced resolutely—inform other poems in which Harrison digs deeper into old ground. "The Heartless Art" is an elegy to a dear friend whose name, Seth, becomes the poet's troubling subject; knowing the difficulty of finding rhymes for "death," Harrison plays on his friend's name and fate in a poem that sends shivers down the spine. But the heart of the book is "The Mother of the Muses," an elegy to the poet's father-in-law, Emmanuel Stratas, who was born in Crete and died in a Toronto home for persons afflicted with memory loss. In thirty-six rhymed octaves, Harrison delves into his father-in-law's life, and his loss of memory of life, as well as the lives and memory losses of others in the home. His depictions of human disintegration—layered, as always, within political and social contexts—are tender and clear. At the end of this powerfully impressive book, the poet tells us once again what, for him, contains the irony of it all:

> In that silent dark I swore I'd make it known,
> while the oil of memory feeds the wick of life
> and the flame from it's still constant and still bright,
> that, come oblivion or not, I loved my wife
> in that long thing where we lay with day like night.

There are no predictably rhymed or metered stanzas in Michael Hofmann's *K.S. in Lakeland: New and Selected Poems*. Hofmann's stylistic métier is structuring perceptions. Hofmann's forms revolve around how he sees his subjects; the impact of his style is heightened by writing around predictable prosody. *K.S. in Lakeland* happily includes almost all of Hofmann's first two books, *Nights in the Iron Hotel* and *Acrimony*,

both published by Faber & Faber, and fourteen poems that
have yet to appear in book form in Britain. Hofmann's reputation in this country has been so far mostly by word of mouth.
Born in West Germany, schooled in Germany, Scotland, Wales,
the United States, and England (where he read Classics and
English Literature at Cambridge University), Hofmann's poems
embody the cosmopolitanism of cross-cultural European modernism. The constant displacements of time, space, and language have created an arresting imagination: The English of
Hofmann's poetry is like no one else's, drawing from the language's Latinate, Germanic, and American sources. I can think
of only two other foreign-born writers this century whose English is imbued with the same wonderfully strange quality—
Joseph Conrad and Vladimir Nabokov.

The "K.S." in the title refers to Kurt Schwitters and the title
poem "Kurt Schwitters in Lakeland." Why "K.S."? The choice is
aesthetic. Schwitters, a progenitor of European expressionism,
died in England—"lakeland"—an exile from the Nazis (who
designated his art "degenerate"). Schwitter's *Merz*—his ongoing
collage form—"was nothing to do with pain or March: / it had
been withdrawn from the *Kommerz-und-Privatbank*," his legatee
poet tells us. Perception was what Schwitters's art was about—
looking at reality from different perspectives, forming them
into expressions of "vision." "K.S."—a further abstraction of
"Kurt Schwitters"—is a reminder that Schwitters and the other
artists to whom the poet expresses allegiance are also a part of
Hofmann's poetic perceptions.

This process of seeing is at the core of Hofmann's poetry.
The self; the careful, emotional figurative depictions of human
conduct; the articulate statements of various social realities and
moral issues; the impressive perspicaciousness of language:
Each is subject and object simultaneously, often within the same
poem, creating a revolving sense of engaged detachment:

> The North Sea was a yeasty, sudsy brown slop.
> My feet jingled on the sloping gravel,
> a crisp musical shingle. My tracks were oval holes
> like whole notes or snowshoes or Dover soles.

Roaring waves of fighters headed back to Bentwaters.
The tide advanced in blunt codshead curves,
ebbed through the chattering teeth of the pebbles.
Jaw jaw. War war.

Sophisticated stuff, yes—but Hofmann never uses any of the cheap sophisticate's tricks. His concern is with the actual world:

Afterwards I smoked a cigarette and lay on my back
panting, as heavy and immobile as my own saliva.
The newspapers preyed on my mind. On the radio,
the National Front had five minutes to put their case.

The fiction of an all-white Albion, deludedness
and control, like my landlady's white-haired old bitch,
who confuses home with the world, peers just inside the door,
and shits trivially in a bend in the corridor.

Mr. Thatcher made his pile by clearing railway lines
with sheep-dip (the millionaire statutory one idea).
When he sold his shares, they grew neglected,
plants break out and reclaim the very pavements . . .

Hofmann is thirty-two. His ability to take on the modernist traditions of several literatures reveals a truly rare talent. And, like any astonishing poetic talent, Hofmann is always several imaginative steps ahead. Read this poet closely to discover what poetry in the English language at the end of this century, and into the next, can do.

Frederick Seidel

From the outset—his first book, *Final Solutions,* was published in 1963 when he was only twenty-seven—Frederick Seidel's strong aesthetic sensibility has clashed with a complex and expansive sense of the world around him. Robert Lowell—never one for exaggerated praise—wrote for the jacket of *Final Solutions* that he suspected "the possibilities of modern poetry have been changed." No doubt Lowell was struck by Seidel's intensely dense, eloquently stylized explorations of a mix of subjects quite never before brought to the foreground of American poetry: the politics of the American empire, moneyed and non-moneyed class, Judaism in the Diaspora, racial oppression and violence. Seidel combined a classical historian's eye for the details of human behavior with a sophisticate's poetics.

Seidel's *Poems, 1959–1979* includes most of *Final Solutions* and Seidel's entire second book *Sunrise,* which received a Lamont award and the National Book Critics Circle Award in 1980. With it, Knopf is publishing Seidel's third book, *These Days.* This would seem to be an opportune time to take a close look at Seidel's work, but both books seem to have dropped into a critical oubliette. A reason for this is, I think, that Seidel's poetry is, on various critical levels, overtly challenging to its reader. Eventually you have to consider what Seidel is up to—which is precisely what he wants. A confronted reader may not care for the provocation, or may just miss the point. Yet other readers—myself among them—may find the complexities, even difficulties, of Seidel's poems enormously compelling in the ways in which they bring you into territories of language that you've never quite heard, nor seen, before.

The poems are often strangely allusive and bizarre. Take, for example, an early poem, "A Negro Judge." The character is described with an almost brutal eye: "Backed up love kills / The loving eye with its quills. / Once, his nerves would have stood and stared, prongs on a mace, / His meatless Jansenist hooked face." What's this all about? There's the hyped-up conceit: nerves, standing and staring, compared to prongs on a mace. (I had to look up what "mace" means; two of the *Oxford Universal Dictionary*'s meanings apply: "a heavy staff or club, either all of metal or metal-headed, often spiked; formerly a weapon of war" or "a staff of office resembling this, borne by certain officials.") A black judge in the early 1960s (there weren't many back then), his nerves, at one time, standing and staring like prongs on a weapon of war or a staff of office resembling it, with a face meatless, Jansenist, and hooked? Is Seidel being ironic? Sardonic? Is the judge intended as a symbol? A metaphor? If so, as a symbol or as a metaphor of what? One suggested answer, two quatrains later, is that the judge has been laid to physical and moral waste by "the lean law" of a "law-hagged America" that "dreams on, with disgust, of a hairy, / Plenary, / Incessant lust, / A God-like black penis, a white buttocks-sized bust." In the poem's final stanzas, there are further tours de force:

> From the Judge's seat, a world of widow's peaks!
> Where the dying defendant shrieks,
> "Your Honor, I believe! Help thou mine unbelief!"
> And slavers with hate and grief.
>
> Plaintiff is awarded the Judge. Passerine,
> Perched on branch and vine,
> Plaintiff spreads its smallish wings—
> Brownish white, whitish brown—and sings.

The poem's meanings expand—switching diction to "Help thou mine unbelief!" by itself shifts meaning. The "plaintiff"? In a criminal case, the plaintiff is the state. In this case, the state, "passerine" (the dictionary again: "of or belonging to the Passeres of about the size of a sparrow, as the Passerine Parrot"), receives, as a judgment in its favor, the judge (in a criminal case, judgment for the state means the defendant is guilty, and subject to incarceration). The result? The American state analogically reduced to a tiny "brownish white, whitish brown" chirping passerine?

Remember this is one poem, from Seidel's first book, written in his twenties, and taken out of context. Every Seidel poem presents similarly arresting, often unanswerable interpretative issues. (I can imagine three or four very different interpretations of "A Negro Judge," each equally plausible.) Take, as another example, "Wanting to Live in Harlem," the opening poem in *Final Solutions.* The poem's structure and language obviously suggest poems from Lowell's *Life Studies;* however, the quality of its expressions cuts against Lowell's. The "I" in the poem does not speak with Lowell's authority—in fact, it doesn't speak with authority at all. The speaker is patently mixed-up: Jewish, from an upper-class St. Louis background, he recalls that as an adolescent his hero, "once I'd read about him, / Was the Emperor Hadrian; my villain, Bar Kochba, / The Jew Hadrian had crushed out at Jerusalem." While his mother is dying—while he sexually fantasizes about a servant, "the young light-skinned colored girl we had then"—the speaker sees

> . . . a world of mirrored darkness! Agonized, elated
> Again years later, I would see it with my naked
> Eye—see Harlem: doped up and heartless,
> Loved up by heroin, running out of veins
> And out of money and out of arms to hold it . . .

Having left St. Louis—having "given up being Jewish, / To be at Harvard just another Greek nose," "almost unarmored"—he "wanted to live in Harlem." The poem's realities—racial consciousness, identity confusion, sexual fantasies, the psychic mirroring of upper and lower classes—reform its Lowell-like dimensions. The self is clearly metaphorized, encoded: We get hints, suggestions, of a personality, a personal history, but these are subsumed by the poem's aesthetic interplays, its confrontations with social taboos—race, sex, class, violence—which are picked up again not only in "A Negro Judge," but throughout the book.

What Seidel's poetry embodies from its beginnings is the modernist conflict between an impressively strong, stylized aesthetic sensibility—which tends to split off into the poet's subjective reality—and the external realities around the poet that inevitably pressure that sensibility. The poems in *Sunrise* pick up the conflict up with a vengeance. The book's opening poem, "1968," demarcates a time of race riots, war, assassinations; its place is a Robert Kennedy for President fund-raiser in Bel Air. The persons attending are "fifty or so of the original" fund-raisers—that is to say, a fraction of the Democratic Party's side of America's moneyed power. "The host, a rock superstar, has / A huge cake of opium, / Which he refers to as 'King Kong.'" The poem's speaker is invisible; what we get are facts, scenes. The invisibility of the speaker creates an appearance of neutrality, but we learn a lot about him from what he chooses to see. What we witness is a world of upper-class politics, sex, and power, depicted through a series of image-layered stanzas. The voice appears removed from it all, but is, in fact, enmeshed: He is the one who sees, at the party's end, "A stranger, and wearing a suit," who "Has to be John the Baptist, / At least, come / To say someone else is coming"—which makes the poet who? Isaiah? If so, he appears to be a pseudo-Isaiah who is witness to an insider's world of partisan politics. We're told the poet's politics directly: Robert Kennedy is eulogized as "the only politician I have loved." "Never again," the poet says in "The New Frontier," "to wake up in the blond / Hush and gauze of that Hyannis sunrise. / Bliss was it / In that dawn to be alive / With our Kool as breakfast, / Make-do pioneers." Still, for an aesthetic mind, politics is no easy matter. Walter Benjamin famously wrote that fascism aestheticized politics and communism politicized art; Seidel wishes to do neither. He admits that he "could love politics for its mind"—a pathos-ridden daydream. But Robert Kennedy—"Shy, compassionate and fierce / Like a figure out of Yeats"—reminds him, "*You're dreaming*," says, "*The gun is mightier than the word*." Kennedy, the politician, pays for his politics with his life; Seidel—the poet, through the mighty word—pays for his politics with his sensibility, with his dreams.

The propulsion toward the aesthetic during a time of brutal social reality makes *Sunrise* quite a book. "Think fast! (Still dreaming?)" the poet says in "Fever." This could be the book's epigraph. The speaker in the poems—when he appears—almost floats through existence, a poetic medium compelled by "This need to look!" Yet, at the same time, life is always there, comprehensively on the counterattack. In the foreground the reader is shown—from different moods and angles—a world of scenes: "Caneton á la presse at the Café Chauveron," the making of a film ("Antonioni walks in the desert shooting / *Zabriskie Point*"), the Finnish Grand Prix at Imatra, Eurotrash millionaires; in the background, "Harlem is still— / Harlem is near . . . The galaxies, / The brainstorms of zero, gasp the fainter / And fainter last breaths of the future." And, both in the background and foreground are women—and, implicitly, a Woman, idealized but unattainable. The tensions are formally expressed by placing different sensations and perceptions on top of one another—syntax resembles the logic and illogic of consciousness. The effects are kinetic, loaded, sometimes requiring second, third, fourth readings. Meanings are more allusive and elusive than in *Final Solutions:* The ante's been upped. Seidel refuses to accept entirely either the world of the aesthete or the world of the politician; each poem expresses a part of the tension between both, probing one way or the other. In the title poem, the speaker immerses himself in images, ideas, and facts bent and compressed within forty roughly metrical, intricately rhymed, nine-line stanzas. The poem creates a mesmerizing effect—political and personal histories are mixed in with, for example, the language of quantum physics—but there's no complete way to describe what the poem means, except perhaps to say that, stanza by stanza, it "thinks fast (still dreaming?)" toward a complex awakening at its end. Clearly, Seidel is venting his aesthetic side, elevating the poem's language to a primary meaning. It's difficult to read the poem all the way through, in part because its synchronousness demands so much attention. "Sunrise" moves well beyond any of the poems in *Final Solutions* into that part of the avant-garde where style predominates.

These Days continues to explore—to deepen and evolve—the fundamental values and motifs of *Final Solutions* and *Sunrise*. It is an extraordinarily powerful book. In some of its poems, Seidel's detached tones are more acrid, critical, and ominously prescient than anything he's ever done—his rhetorical, impersonal, didactic side coming on strong. There are "the CIA boys" in "Our Gods" with "EYES / ONLY clearance and profiles like arrowheads":

> They were never home, even when they were there.
> Public servants in secret are not servants,
> Either. They were our gods working all night
> To make Achilles' beard fall out and prop up
> The House of Priam, who by just pointing sent
> A shark fin gliding down a corridor,
> Almost transparent, like a water-mark.

There are conceits as taunting as that which concludes "Empire": "Rank as the odor in urine / Of asparagus from the night before, / This is empire waking drunk, and remembering in the dark." A profound, resonant tenderness—still detached, but almost religiously reposed—informs other poems, in particular "Flame" and "The Blue-Eyed." Although the images remembered in the first stanza of "Flame" are "like waking from a fever," the poet wakens to darkness purer than that of any of the poems in *Sunrise*:

> And then the moon steps from the cypresses and
> A wave of feeling breaks, phosphorescent—
> Moonlight, a wave hushing on a beach.
> In the dark, a flame goes out. And then
> The afterimage of a flame goes out.

"The Blue-Eyed Doe" is a middle-aged child's lullaby-like elegy to his mother. "They'll shave her head for the lobotomy, / They'll cut her brain, they'll kill her at the source," the poet says, concluding with an unabashed aesthetic and moral response:

> The son who lifts his sword above Art Hill;
> Who holds it almost like a dagger but
> In blessing, handle up, and not to kill;
> Who holds it by the blade that cannot cut.

There are also poems (the last five, beginning with "AIDS Days," in particular) that push Seidel's aesthetic toward a strangely conceived, emotionally, socially, and religiously bound . . . I don't quite know what to call it—a hyper-surrealism? Releasing meanings through reconstructed images of earlier themes, Seidel reveals submerged realms. Wildly fractured—at times sometimes bordering on the nonsensical—the poems explode with sardonic sting. In "Gethsemane," the poet postures himself against "the crowd," adopting the ludicrous role of the last prophet, a Jesus abandoned by man, woman, and God, priapically mad, sweating not blood but words. "The Last Poem in the Book" reminds the reader that Seidel has never left the ultimate world of the poem. Not surprisingly, it provides no closure: "I'm coming now. / I can't breathe. / I'm coming now to the conclusion that / Without a God. I'm coming now to the conclusion."

My conclusion? In American poetry today there is no one with Frederick Seidel's sheer ambition, comprehensive sense of our times, sophistication, nerve, and skill. His unique embodiment of the complexities of the clashes between poetic and social truths makes him one of the most vital and important poets we have, wielding poems almost like daggers, but in blessing.

Enzensberger's *Kiosk*

I

Kiosk is the first book of poems by Hans Magnus Enzensberger published in the United States since *The Sinking of the Titanic* appeared in 1980. *Kiosk* was published in Germany in 1995. The Sheep Meadow Press is also publishing Enzensberger's *Selected Poems*, which includes poems from six of Enzensberger's books.

The poems in *Kiosk* and *Selected Poems* are translated into English by Michael Hamburger and, in some instances (most notably the poems from *The Sinking of the Titanic*), by Enzensberger himself. Hamburger has translated Enzensberger's poetry since the mid-1960s. In 1968, he edited and introduced a selection of Enzensberger's poems published by Penguin in Britain, in its Modern European Poets series. The book was among the first in the series, which introduced to English-speaking readers—often for the first time in book form—Eugenio Montale, Fernando Pessoa, Anna Akhmatova, Paul Celan, Aimé Césaire, Yannos Ritsos, Cesare Pavese, Antonio Machado, Salvatore Quasimodo, Nelly Sachs, Zbigniew Herbert, Johannes Bobrowski, Miroslav Holub, Vasko Popa, Gunnar Ekelof, and Yehuda Amichai, among others.

Hamburger—who, with Christopher Middleton, had edited the widely-read anthology *Modern German Poetry 1910–1960,* and, later, wrote one of the finest books written on modernist aesthetics, *The Truth of Poetry: Tensions in Modern Poetry from Baudelaire to the 1960s*—noted in his introduction that Enzensberger's first book of poems, *In Defense of the Wolves,* was published in 1957, only one year after both Bertolt Brecht and Gottfried Benn died (Brecht in East Berlin, Benn in West Berlin; Enzensberger lived in West Berlin at the time). Hamburger's reference to Brecht and to Benn is critical to an understanding of Enzensberger's work. "I don't want to talk about my biography, but, for me, the mere fact of being born in 1929 is practically determining, politically speaking," Enzensberger told Martin Chalmers in a 1989 interview in the *New Left Review*. One might also say that the fact of being born in 1929 is, for a German poet, also determining, poetically speaking: One of the effects of the endless horrors of the Nazi regime is what it did to German poetry. Here, Benn and Brecht are typical. Both were condemned, and their work banned, by the Nazis because of their aesthetics. Brecht, as a communist, was forced into exile, for fear of being killed. In 1933, Benn became involved with the National Socialists, but, shortly afterward, became not only disillusioned, but morally appalled by them. In 1936, his work was censored as degenerate. Benn stayed in Germany, withdrawing as a writer but continuing to practice medicine and to write, with no expectation of ever being published again. Intensely intellectual, enormously erudite, prodigiously gifted with language, Benn was imaginatively obsessed with the relationship between reality and the human brain. Truth existed in the inner act of forming reality, and then expressing it in an object of art. The working out of the tension between inner and outer realities is the constant issue in Benn's poetry and his prose. The only things that matter—the only things which, in reality, are true—are the external objects of human creation and the deep human processes by which they are made, what Benn called "the world of expression." Although Brecht also probed the relationship between external and internal reality, he believed that the internalization of subjective feeling (as expressed, for example, in the anthrosophism of poets like Christian Morgenstern, Rainer Marie Rilke, and, even, George Trakl) was morally (and therefore aesthetically) wrong. Brecht judged a work of art (here his critique was Marxist) by how it expresses the effects of history and economics—the effect of politics—on individual and collective human life.

Though far apart both ideologically and aesthetically, Benn and Brecht were similar in several respects. Both, for example, were obsessed with the problem of alienation. Both also recognized colloquial speech as the source of writing. Enzensberger, by the fact of being German, inherited Benn's and Brecht's pre-occupation with alienation. He also would take from them the aesthetic conviction that every form of writing is, in the first in-stance, the vocal speech of one's time. But Enzensberger would not make the same imaginative mistake that both Benn and Brecht made. Each, in his own way, had tried to collectivize an intensely individualized, even deterministic aesthetic, into a po-litical theory, and each failed terribly, often to the detriment of his art. Enzensberger would, by necessity, figure out in his own way how to express the fundamental modernist conflict between the aesthetic and the political.

II

Enzensberger's work had, by the late sixties, achieved interna-tional recognition. In Germany, he was considered the most am-bitiously innovative poet of his generation. His critical talents also emerged in other forms. In 1960, he edited an anthology of international poetry, *Museum of Modern Poetry,* in which he helped define the critical terrain of poetic modernism. Four years later, Adorno, in a declaration that spread throughout the intellectual and artistic circles of Europe, introduced Enzens-berger to an overflowing crowd at Frankfurt University as "the only critic that Germany had." In fact, Adorno added, "other than a few other scattered efforts," Enzensberger's was the only criticism worth his while to read. By the early seventies, Enzen-berger had published three more books of poetry: *Language of the Country* in 1960, *Braille* in 1964, and *Poems 1955–1970* in 1971. He had also by then translated poetry into German from the French, English, Spanish, Italian, Swedish, and Russian; translated and edited a volume of selected poems by Williams Carlos Williams; and written dozens of introductions and com-mentaries. In 1972, he published a play on the Bay of Pigs inva-sion, *The Havana Inquiry,* and a documentary novel on Spanish anarchism, *The Short Summer of Anarchy: Life and Death of Buena-ventura Durruti.* In 1974, a selection of his essays from the fifties, sixties, and early seventies appeared for the first time in English translation in *The Consciousness Industry and Political Crimes.*

Mausoleum: Thirty-Seven Ballads from the History of Progress—translated into English by Joachim Neugroschel—appeared in the United States in 1976. The book's title and subtitle are not without irony: The thirty-seven poems in it are presented as a series of biographies; each poem's title is, simply, the initials of the person's name, followed by the dates during which they lived. Each piece tracks the lives of men (the fact that there are no women is also not without irony) who have affected the moral, political, and economic "progress" of human beings, operating on multiple levels of meaning, employing different types of historical and technical jargon and diction. Two years later, in 1978, *The Sinking of the Titanic* was published in Germany (with the subtitle *A Comedy*). The English translation, by Enzensberger, appeared in 1980 (without the subtitle). The book has become an international classic. In it, Enzensberger uses the *Titanic* as a metaphor to reveal a multitude of aesthetic, historical, cultural, political, moral, economic, and, even, biographical issues. His translations of his own poems in *Titanic* into English are stunning, sounding as if they were written not only by a native speaker, but by a poet inventing a pitch-perfect colloquial language somewhere between English and American.

In 1980, Enzensberger founded the international journal *Transatlantik* (in 1964, he founded and edited *Kursbach*—in German, "timetable" or "railroad guide"). He also published *The Fury of Disappearance,* a book of poems. During the eighties and into the nineties, his reputation continued to grow. *Europe, Europe: Forays into a Continent*—a best-seller in Europe—was published in the United States in 1989. Two other books of essays, *Political Crumbs* and *Mediocrity and Delusion,* appeared in 1990 and 1992. *Civil Wars: From L.A. to Bosnia,* published in the United States in 1994, included three essays, "Civil War," "Europe in Ruins," and "The Great Migration." *Zig-Zag: The Politics of Culture and Vice-Versa,* a selection of essays (some previously not translated) appeared in 1998. Also published in 1998 was the translation into English of *The Number Devil: A Mathematical Adventure*—another best-seller in Europe—a book ostensibly written for children, but, not surprisingly, defying generic classification.

III

"Writing should be a way of discovering something, not of proving what you already know," Enzensberger emphasized in his interview with Martin Chalmers. The act of discovery, of opening oneself up to experience—the activity of seeking knowledge and meaning—is, in fact, what defines the imaginative landscape of Enzensberger's work. For Enzensberger, the primary act of discovery is the poem; each poem contains its own universe of language, its own act of anarchy. A poem's only limitation is its form—which, too, is, in the deepest sense, created freely, igniting in its readers what we think and feel apart from the manipulations of the mass culture (which Enzensberger famously coined "the consciousness industry").

Enzensberger has consistently explored a poem's formal space. One way that he implicitly circumscribes poetry is by prose. For Enzenberger—to paraphrase Montale—poetry, vocally, is that which tends toward prose yet at the same time refutes it; the ways by which a poem resists prose are what constitute its form. The formal measures used to refute prose—meter, rhyme, shape, lineation, punctuation, syntax, vocal pressures, and juxtapositions—are to be used freely. Enzensberger rejects the notion of genre, the categorization—the limitation—of a text by its form or content; the processes by which form and content are created must be open, not closed. Reading, for a writer, is a productive, not an interpretative, act; the writer recomposes the form and content of other writers' texts into something as new and different as what is going on in the streets. Enzensberger has openly praised, for example, the free-form combination of dialogue, descriptive narrative, quotation, paradox, and, even, elements of fiction, in the journalism of Edmund Wilson, Janet Flanner, Martha Gellhorn, and among his peers, Bruce Chatwin and Ryszard Kapuscinski. Even his preoccupation with German identity and with German politics is a form of open thinking, an attempt to come to grips with what are immediate and necessary historical, cultural, and moral issues. But, when modes of thought and expression begin to narrow, Enzensberger shifts ground. He has spoken of himself—

like Ibsen and Strindberg—as a provincial on the periphery of imperial and military power. For a German at the end of the century, this is, of course, said with irony, but it is irony with a point. Creative energy does not necessarily result from living in the midst of military or economic power. The poet is always on the periphery, part of the circle of things, yet, at the same time, apart from them. Enzensberger's ability to participate in present affairs through eye-witness observation, and his capacity to comprehend surface realities in a world increasingly mediated and commodified by the raw force of technological change, co-exist with an equally compelling need to discover what we know and what we are as human beings. The feeling created in a work of verbal art by these often conflicting needs borders on the phenomenological. A work of literature has something about it that transcends its politics and its aesthetics.

Enzensberger has recently been interested in the work of written art as anachronism. In a time of overwhelming mass external stimuli, the gene-pool of the culture, he says, is kept alive by the artist. A poet pays attention not only to what we don't know: She or he is also in touch with what Enzensberger calls the "patchwork" of different times that exist in each one of us. Our minds contain things that do not correspond to one another in any present sense of time. The poet appreciates what is topical, but, at the same time, sabotages it by resisting what appears to be, and by holding onto the endlessly deep sources of time that each of us carries around inside us. A work of written art releases the pressure of the paradox—the same release of paradoxical pressure that Walter Benjamin likened to the Messiah.

IV

Kiosk is made up of four parts of roughly equal length: "Historical Patchwork," "Mixed Feelings," "Diversions under the Cranium," and "In Suspense." The sense of the "patchwork" of times in each of us, collectively and individually, sets the tone of the book. Enzensberger creates a kind of imaginative transversal of the present and the past, the epistemological and ontological pressures generated by the collisions of different realities and perceptions. The fundamental issue of the "inner" and the "outer" is not only consistently reenacted, but deepened: Each poem includes a patchwork of motifs, a mixture of voices and types of languages and dictions—expressions of the intricacies of both the historical world and the activity of the mind.

Often a poem will switch, or seem to switch, speakers: We're in aesthetic realms similar to those of Gertrude Stein, Samuel Beckett, John Ashbery. This, for example, is the opening stanza of "On the Algebra of Feelings":

> I often have the feeling (intense,
> obscure, indefinable etc)
> that the I is not a fact
> but a feeling
> I can't get rid of.

The overall feeling is phenomenological—the interplay between surface and depth, both in the world, and in the mind of the individual. The results, always surprising, are elevating: By "a flight of ideas" (the title of a poem in each part of the book) we are brought toward something other than our subjective selves or what the mass culture is telling us we are.

Kiosk opens with the title poem:

> At the nearest corner
> the three elderly sisters
> in their wooden booth.
> Blithely they offer
> murder poison war
> to a nice clientele
> for breakfast.
>
> Fine weather today. Homeless folk
> eating dog biscuits. Property owners
> choking in villas
> beneath Tanagra figurines,
> and other living creatures
> who at sunrise punctually
> disappear in banks,

weird as the mammoth
with its ringed tusks
and the praying mantis.
They don't disturb me.
I too like to do
my shopping at the Fates.

Right away we're in the world of expression, of metaphor, of
morality. At the nearest corner—on the street—the Fates are
selling the times that we live in: murder, poison, war. This time:
fine weather, the poor eating dog biscuits, property owners
choking in villas beneath exotic, expensive, objects of art, and
the financiers, weird as (metaphor!) the elephant, as the praying mantis. But the "I" (not a fact, but a feeling) is buying, too:
the morning newspaper; his—our—fate. All that you have to do
is stay with him as he leaves the kiosk and takes you word by
word, line by line, poem by poem, through yet another master-
piece of poetry.

Kiosk ends with "The Entombment." Like "Kiosk," it has three
stanzas:

Our mortal frame,
they call it.
But what did it hold?
The psychologist will say:
Your psyche.
Your soul,
the priest.
Your personality,
the personnel manager.

Furthermore,
there's the anima,
the imago, the daemon,
the identity and the Ego,
not to mention the Id
and the Super-Ego.

The butterfly which is to rise
from this very mixed lot
belongs to a species
about which nothing is known.

In 1963, Enzensberger wrote the introduction to the poems of Nelly Sachs (the introduction appeared in translation in *O the Chimneys,* a joint publication, in 1967, of The Jewish Publication Society of America and Farrar, Straus and Giroux). In it, he speaks of the "character" of Sachs's poems. Sachs's poems are hard but transparent—they never dissolve in the weak solution of interpretation. Though not easy to read, they are not difficult in a technical sense, nor by calculation. The metaphoric codes that Sachs constructs are not hermetic. She doesn't make language puzzles. Her indeterminateness contains a sense of enigma, of paradox. The poems unfold themselves gradually, by and through their language. Nothing in them is isolated. From one poem to the next, concrete detail is reiterated, until the entire work's connotations are established. Even a poem's words and images are subject to this transformation. One image, in particular, revealed throughout the work, is expressive of the process itself: the image of the butterfly. "Inscription, butterfly, metamorphoses, flight," Enzensberger writes. "As these elements of her poetry unfold themselves and intertwine, so do all the words that stand in this book. Wherever the reader begins, with the metaphor of hair and fire, the hunter and the hunted, sea and wings, or finger and shoe: from every point the 'words' mesh of veins' will open up to him, and even the most daring telescoping of expression, the cryptically condensed stanza, will become transparent to him when he traces the multifariousness of this coral reef of images. This poetry is also cabalistic in this linguistic sense: as the world of a magical *ars combinatora* that knows how to grasp even the incommensurable ever more lightly the more remote it is."

Inscription, butterfly, metamorphoses, flight: the poem as release from the depths of our "entombment," the transformation into something incommensurable—something grasped ever more lightly the more remote it is—something about which nothing, other than what it is, can be known. A deep release not only from the pressures and paradoxes of German poetry at the end of the century, but—with a few other scattered efforts—a release also from the pressures and paradoxes that exist deep within the art of poetry itself—the same release that Walter Benjamin likened to the Messiah.

"Our Lives Are Here"

Notes from a Journal, Detroit, 1975

January 8

A cold, damp gray afternoon. Our second week in our apartment in the Alden Park, near the river. Neither of us can imagine living in this city away from its river, its strait. Looking out our kitchen window at the ash tree in the backyard of Detroit Towers, a flock of small birds. On Belle Isle—a bus, a few cars. The "Two Brothers" smokestacks on the Edison power plant spilling smoke horizontally, southward, to Canada . . . the river a silver-green. From beyond Belle Isle, the sound of freighters' horns—a reminder that this is one of the world's major ports . . .

The commute to Ann Arbor to law school four times a week . . . the remainder of my time here. I want to keep two kinds of notes: a chronicle of events—a "history"; and *pensées,* perceptions, *logoi,* on various subjects—on poetry, on law, on Detroit, and on my own poetry and poetics . . . ongoing poetic memoranda . . .

January 15

Mid-January. "No hopeful signs for the economy" . . . "as Detroit goes so goes the Nation." More and more empty houses and stores, For Lease and For Sale signs. ". . . as long as the Supplemental Unemployment Benefits pay holds out"—but then what? And to think that not even two years ago one of the major issues in the shops was involuntary overtime!

Ways to cope, the instinct to survive. Our common past experience has taught us that social breakdown eventually erupts into externalized or internalized forms of horror and violence. Survival requires that we forget—which is why, for the poet, it is literally vital to try to remember, at any cost, what is crucial and good. A theological concept: The act of memory becomes an act of faith; if whatever is good is to be revealed (and, therefore, exist), the poet must remain vigilantly capable of recognizing it . . .

February 4
Fascination with place, the effect on our individual and collective selves. "Detroit" allows (or, more accurately, demands) that I consider myself in the contexts of my personal and family histories, and in the contexts of histories of America—American histories of "industry," of "labor," and of "capital." "Social metaphors"—material for poetry.

February 18
Dusk. By the river. No smoke from the two Uniroyal smokestacks—an eerie image against the dark gray light and the dark green river. The memory—nearly two years ago now—the Chrysler Clairpointe factory, before I began law school, standing on the loading dock with Bill Leuvanos, breaktime, the sun bright, the upper half of the sky clear blue, the lower half its perpetual burned-earth dust. I said, "It's pretty today." Leuvanos replied, "Detroit is never pretty." I asked him to tell me, then, what kind of day it was. "Detroit is never pretty," he repeated.

Earlier this afternoon at the Biff's Coffee Shop on Jefferson, a woman, destitute, a tattered blue dress above her knees, red socks at her ankles, laughing at two policemen. Later, in Memorial Park, the flock of water fowl lifting in unison, first parallel to the river, then upward toward Lake St. Clair. The touch of warmer weather in the air . . . smells of wet grass . . . river smells . . .

March 1
This morning, at the Belle Isle Casino, a long conversation with a retired autoworker, Tom Grantley. He worked in factories—Packard, Kaiser, General Motors Transmission—for over thirty years. He saw my law books and said: "I see that you are studying law. Maybe I can tell you about this." He killed a man last October. "On Halloween night, I went and helped this woman I know

who owns a pharmacy on Oakland at Clay—I work there three hours and she gives me twenty dollars. Early in the evening, two young men come in, look around—I get suspicious. They leave, but I remember them. When we close, my woman friend asks me to accompany her to her car. She hands me a pistol—to protect us, she said. She wanted me to stay with her while she waited for a friend who was at church across the street so that they could drive home together. When she opens the car door, she turns and then screams, 'Look! He's coming up behind you!' One of the men I'd noticed earlier was coming toward me. I dodged. He went against the car, rebounded off it, then grabbed my woman friend and put a gun to her back. I had the pistol—I knew how to use it—I was in the service—and shot him before he knew what hit him, right through his heart. It all happened so fast. He ran a whole block before he fell, dead. The police came, told me not to worry. They said I was lucky, that what usually happens is the victims are told to get into the car, and then robbed and killed. One policeman said it was too bad that I didn't have the opportunity to kill the other man, too." He lost twelve pounds in the week after it happened. He's been unable to forget it—"I can't ever forget it." He's waiting for spring—"to get away from all this." He loves to fish—he intends to go to Canada when the weather breaks. "Mine's not been an easy life. I deserve some peace, some retirement."

March 22
At Biff's on Jefferson—he's in his early twenties, talks to everyone at the counter. "I live day by day. I can't worry about the unemployment." We all look away from him. He's been laid off from Chrysler for eight months. Outside the sky—blue, shaded red. Dusk. The air cold. I step into it, breathe deeply, fill with my own nostalgia—yet the sense of the present, the oppressive present, is here always . . .

April 7
"World-Detroit-self"—to work through the potential interrelationships. To keep in mind Camus's note on Faulkner: "To write," Faulkner said, "you must let the great primary truths take root in you and direct your work toward one of them or

toward all of them at the same time"; and, "When writers stop being afraid then they will write works again that endure." To confront fear—both our personal and our collective fears—is integral to any aesthetic.

June 4

Extremely humid, rainy morning. Black clouds, black sky. Almost nine o'clock. At the Ram's Horn, a coffee shop on Cadillac Square, about two blocks from the office. The waitress is telling a customer about a woman who "comes in here wearing a Siamese cat around her neck" . . .

Poetry. Read the King James Bible, the histories, for narrative structure.

Work—not bad, at least not yet. Rabin thinks about money first, power and status second—but what did I expect?

June 5

In Grand Circus Park. A woman tells two other women seated beside her on a nearby park bench what she ate yesterday, "a piece of leftover cornbread and a heated Hostess cake." Last night on television she watched a rerun of the Tony Orlando Christmas Show. "He had his grandmother with him. He's sentimental, you know. He was holding her hand and singing Silent Night. I had to cry. My husband—he used to kick the hell out of me because I cry so much. He'd say, 'Why the hell are you crying?'" All three then talked about how much they cry. "Holy Toledo!" one exclaims—one o'clock in the afternoon, downtown Detroit, a slight drizzle suddenly filling the thick humid air.

June 10

This morning, at breakfast, at the Howard Johnson's on Washington Boulevard and Michigan Avenue, a conversation between a man about my age and the waitress, older, about thirty-five. He intends to take a course in Humanities. "I hear it's easy and real good. Includes things like psychology, sociology." He then moves over beside a man wearing a blazer with a Detroit Lions emblem on the front pocket, speaking in a self-consciously lower voice, almost a whisper, until, suddenly, he spills his coffee. An eruption. He laughs loudly, nervously . . . I asked the waitress how she was this morning. "Holding on," she replied. She's not crazy about her job. She's tried others—"community services," for example—but "couldn't pay the rent." She asks me what I do. "I do law," I answer, apologetically. "It's competitive," I continue, "dog eat dog"; I slide my index finger across the front of my neck to prove my point. I tell her that yesterday my work was "purely bureaucratic," then repeat the phrase. She notices my Weldon Kees book. I mention that I'm also a poet—the conversation stops. As I get up to leave a few minutes later, she says, "Well, Wallace Stevens was vice president of an insurance company, Prudential, I think." My immediate reaction is to correct her—Stevens was a lawyer, and that's how he became a vice president, for Hartford, not Prudential . . . but I don't. I don't think to ask her how she knows or cares about Wallace Stevens!

Last night at the river—orange, white, pink mists. Stars. A magical quality to the air that seemed to make Belle Isle, the Bridge, the river, the Canadian shoreline, and the "great factories" almost palpable, accessible to touch . . .

June 13

A cool, windy green summer morning. Friday. Ran into Przywara on Woodward Avenue just after I got off the bus. I hadn't seen him since we graduated from high school. He's a lawyer with a small firm in the First National Bank Building; he does corporate—"mostly securities"—work. He graduated from U of M law school right before I began. He hasn't lost any of his elemental distrust of . . . everything—but he's so genuinely skeptical that it still becomes him. He's kept up on his Greek—Homeric and Attic (which he studied at Holy Cross). He's been reading Pindar in the original—"as an exercise of the mind." He says that it gives him an advantage in drafting complex securities agreements.

Yesterday, after dinner, a long drive through the eastside. The blight—Van Dyke, Harper, Gratiot, Vernor, Mack Avenue—whole blocks as if bombed during an old war, never rebuilt—three, four miles from where we live. Then, out Gratiot, northeast, the neighborhoods near Denby High—rows of small brick houses, well-kept, with trimmed, handsome yards. Small stores, a lot of bars. Occasional For Sale signs.

This morning, my past in this city swelled again in me, its strife a part of my body, part of my nature.

"History is bunk," Henry Ford said. *Bunk*—the sound of a piece of metal falling on a concrete factory floor. We must forget, mustn't we—and we do, until what is forgotten is sublimated into terrible vengeance. ". . . and so goes the Nation."

August 7

Cesare Pavese's essay "The Poet's Craft" . . . The issues that he raises—the "demands of technique" and how these demands coincide and relate to the narrative poem . . . The importance that he places on technically justifying his poetry. His statement that he knew, "naturally," that there are no traditional meters in an absolute sense—that every poet re-creates in himself or herself "interior rhythms of the imagination. I worked out the rhythms of my poetry by repeating them to myself. Gradually I discovered the intrinsic laws of this meter and my poetry fell into three unvarying categories which I regard as the rhythm of my imagination." I would add that the "unvarying categories" Pavese speaks of are, in essence, *formal* categories, a poet's *forms* . . .

Pavese. Camus. They read their worlds well, in the sense that Simone Weil speaks of "reading" the world . . . a classical impulse to understand, to "make conscious"—the creation of a *poesis* . . .

November 13

Yesterday: bone-chilling cold that the landscape seemed to equal. The single smokestack near Eastern Market; St. Josephat's towers seen from the Chrysler Freeway; the burned-out warehouse in old Poletown surrounded by acres of weeds . . .

How much lost—how much hidden, buried, forgotten. How much fear absorbs the capacity to see and accept . . .

> Where is the great light my grandfather left behind?
> My life is here . . .

Write poetry that has value, that has the power to resist oppressive power—poetry that speaks directly to others, with love . . .

December 12

Friday night, late. Just finished outlining the Enterprise Organizations course . . . Now to review three or four chapters of Secured Transactions. Floating liens—how a lender protects itself from bone fide purchasers . . .

A freezing cold night of snow. Papers and books all over the apartment. The wind is howling over the river. Every once and awhile I look out to see if it's still snowing . . . it still is. What if I took the time to work on poetry that I take to study law—but no, of course, the intensity required to write poems must be differently directed. An idea for a poem (inspiration these days comes in ideas)—a poem about one of the hungry murdered during the 1933 "Hunger March" on the Ford Rouge plant, an elegy. I narrate what he felt—the despair and hope that led him to risk and to lose his life. This came to me this afternoon driving back from Ann Arbor—on Wyoming, beside The Rouge. The Rouge River appeared frozen, but was simply a drab, concrete gray. The smell of sulfur was heavy; the smoke—as it poured from the eight smokestacks—adding to the massive quality and weight of the snow clouds . . .

December 22

Finished with exams . . . next, the bar exam.

A day spent mostly riding buses—down Warren, downtown, then back, to get Nancy's ignition key, because mine had broken in the frozen car door lock. On the bus, an old Irishman wearing a white shirt with a starched collar suddenly began to talk to me—within minutes I knew that he was retired, that he worked in auto factories and small tool-and-die shops from 1925 to 1960 ("been retired sixteen years"), and that he had never worked long enough at any one place to have received a pension. While waiting near Crowley's for the bus downtown, a fifteen-year-old girl, slightly cross-eyed, biting her lower lip self-consciously, ashamed of how she looks. The man waiting for the bus in line before me—waist-length naval jacket, small blue cap, unshaven, protruded jaw—every five minutes or so cursed, "Goddamn bus is late." We wait thirty minutes, but it seems twice as long. The air freezing cold—Detroit freezing cold gray . . . The ride back, on Gratiot—hundreds of stores closed forever. On to Warren, at the

Chrysler Kercheval plant, a worker, leaning from a third-story window. Another worker gets off the bus, running to the gate—he's late for work. A worker in his grease-stained apron on the loading dock, outside for a smoke. A "motor city"—eventually we come to the factories. All of us—the girl, eighteen, on the bus reading an old paperback edition of *Crime and Punishment*; the respectable liars; the lost; the fuck-offs; the cool crooks; the blessed—all of us, our lives are here.

John Ashbery and Adrienne Rich

In late 1936, Wallace Stevens delivered, at Harvard, his first public lecture on poetry. Shaken, as was everyone, by the Great Depression, Stevens spoke of the fact that "politics" had become "nearer to each of us" as a result of "the pressure of the contemporaneous." But, Stevens contended, "in poetry the subject is not the contemporaneous, because that is only the nominal subject, but the poetry of the contemporaneous." Though, at first glance, no one would deny that John Ashbery's and Adrienne Rich's poetry appears distinctive, each poet's work, at its core, remakes—one might even say revisions—Stevens's insight. Both poets have compulsively explored the persistent pressure that late-twentieth-century American life imposes upon a poet's fundamental need to create. *Flow Chart* and *An Atlas of the Difficult World* prove the point: In them, Ashbery and Rich project their respective poetries of living reality more magnanimously than ever.

John Ashbery's poetry has always been, if anything, contemporary. For Ashbery, the concept is defined by a modernist tradition that goes back not only to Stevens but to Gertrude Stein, who believed that a writer's language should capture as much of a sense of the present as possible. That's what Ashbery tries to do: Everything, including what it means to write poetry, is fair imaginative game. But that isn't all. Ashbery also possesses a highly sophisticated, idiosyncratic feeling for the avant-garde. Combining configurations of present existence with indications of how meaning is discovered and formed, he imagines contemporaneity in its fullest sense. Every Ashbery book approaches the contemporary world—and what poetry is within it—differently; yet every book aspires toward, and achieves, some idea of what we experience and know. For Ashbery, language contains multiple meanings; his poetry reflects—you might even say bears witness to—this. Subjects replace subjects; the "I" stays in a state of referential and definitional flux. Various feelings are expressed continuously through different types of voices arranged within beautifully formed, yet syntactically and colloquially diverse sentences. You may disagree with how, in a given poem, Ashbery chooses to figure it all out; an autotelic imagination, after all, has a propensity for excess. But Ashbery knows his limits: Part of what his poetry does is stay ahead of what you might be thinking about it, consistently creating an ever-new poetic space.

Flow Chart portrays the essence of Ashbery's process. The title indicates the book-length poem's central preoccupation: Like a flow chart, it may be read according to what the reader desires. If the title's metaphorical signal is somehow missed, the poet reminds you, at the end of the first of the poem's six parts, what his intentions are: "But if it interests you / you can browse through this catalog and, who knows, perhaps come up with a solution that will apply / to your complicated case. Just conceivably, or perhaps you know someone better informed / in the higher echelons where the view is distant and severe, / the ground blue as steel." The passage is one of many that reveal the book's recurring awareness of its own pursuits: *Flow Chart* is a catalogue, which Ashbery presents as endlessly expansive and open to interpretation, encompassing within its subject matter—well, as much as the poet may imagine.

Yet, although you can't quite locate what *Flow Chart* is "about," certain subjects are insistently noticed: the nature of the city ("Still in the published city but not yet / overtaken by a new form of despair, I ask / the diagram: is it the foretaste of pain / it might easily be?" the poem begins); memory; death (of a mother in particular); religion; art; politics and work; and a revelatory preoccupation with love and love talk. The poem sounds like a diary of how we talk about ourselves and our world:

> There isn't much you can do, and it's a little darker. Tell it
>   the time. And on no account lose your bearings
> unless you want to wash up like a piece of polyester at the
>   gulf's
> festering edge. That tanker took on more water. The
>   consensus was that there *would be* a

symposium, if anyone could be found to host it. Meanwhile
   things are getting a little better
on that front too, which includes romance.

You're supposed to take the poet at his word—read the poem
where and how you want, look or listen for language that
catches your ear, eye, or sensibility. Reading it is like listening to
an intriguing conversation, or returning to a piece of music
whose powers you're convinced of, to listen to parts of it, or the
whole in relation to the parts—like focusing, for example, on
the interstices between abstraction and figuration in a modernist painting.

Written for the most part in long (flowing) conversational,
almost meditative lines (a form of personal tonal talk that Ashbery has been refining for years), the poem is composed into
sections that are, more accurately, verse paragraphs. The language has a formal feel to it that diffuses the vocal intimacies
just enough—you never quite know how attached to the speaker
or listener the person speaking is:

   I don't know where this one came in—but wait,
   it is of myself I speak, and I do know! But the looks I got
      convinced me I was someone
   else as I walked in, not at all sure of myself or (rightly, as it
      turned out) of
   the reception I would be getting.

Because of the feel of the language and all that it maintains,
reading *Flow Chart* provides its pleasures wherever you choose
them. You come away when you've had enough satisfaction and
go back when you want more:

   Any day now you must start to dwell in it,
   the poetry, and for this, grave preparations must be made,
      the walks of sand
   raked, the rubble wall picked clean of dead vine stems, but
      what
   if poetry were something else entirely, not this purple
      weather
   with the eye of a god attached, that sees inward and
      outward?

"Voices of autumn in full, heavy summer; / algae spangling a pool. A lot remains to be done, doesn't it? / I haven't even begun to turn myself inside-out yet," the poem says near its end, after having turned its radically comprehensive voices both outside and in.

Adrienne Rich's contemporaneity is less covert. Acutely aware of moral and social effects, and blessed with an extraordinary critical intelligence, Rich, since the early 1960s, has written poetry that runs counter to the language of a certain Romantic tradition which is both self-centered and noncritical. From her earliest work, Rich has projected her poetry as a form of thought (for example, "The Diamond Cutters," the title poem of her second book, concentrates on the act of creation). In the 1960s, Rich's poetry became aware of its critical powers: Poetry becomes a means through which forms of inhuman power can be exposed. Needless to say, Rich's aesthetic is tied to her political sensibility. She defines herself as a socialist and a feminist, identities that have provided her with a strong and sometimes doctrinal language. Yet Rich remains unique in the ways in which she applies her political insights to the practice of modernist poetry. Most "socially aware" or "socially engaged" poets settle for a poetry of worked-over diction and a sloppiness of sentiment critically indistinguishable from the second-rate nineteenth-century versifiers. Rich pulls from—as every poet does—her own experience, but she is not aesthetically interested in portraying an autobiography. Rich looks at herself and her subject matter hard, pushing out the complexities of human behavior through an "I" who is essentially functional, yet, at the same time, both personal and social. For Rich, the poet, inside a wrecked society, must will an imagined common language to get to forms of human love, which are, for her, the central subjects of any personal or social order. Poetry of ideological commitment must enter the heart and mind and become as real as one's body, as vital as life itself. That's what makes it poetry. In Stevens's terms, Rich's subject is above all the poetry of contemporary political economy and morality. Her emphasis on the autonomy of the art engenders an irony akin to Bertolt Brecht's. Her poetry's passionate turning back into language itself—within a society that overwhelms it with its terrors—gives Rich's work its persistent and undeniable power.

An Atlas of the Difficult World possesses this power throughout. The book's title picks up a recurrent motif in Rich's work ("The words are maps," she wrote in her famous 1972 poem "Diving Into the Wreck"): the creation of a cartography as a metaphor for poetic language. The mapping-out is, in the first instance, an aesthetic statement. Then, Rich projects—as she always does—her territory. Whereas her last two books, *Your Native Land, Your Life* and *Time's Power: Poems 1985–1988*, took on, respectively, the relationship between poetry and the body, and poetry and time, *An Atlas* chooses as its focal point "the *difficult* world," as opposed to other "worlds" the poet may have chosen.

The focus of the undertaking allows Rich to be especially expansive. The book has two parts. Part one is the title poem, comprised of thirteen sections. To paraphrase what Rich has said of Elizabeth Bishop's poetry, the poem critically and consciously explores marginality, power and powerlessness, with great beauty and sensuousness, and characteristic clarity as well. "I am struck to earth," the poet says, as she reveals the worlds of hatred, suffering, and violence that try our senses of light and darkness, and beauty and love. The writing is graceful and gorgeous:

> Within two miles of the Pacific rounding
> this long bay, sheening the light for miles
> inland, floating its fog through redwood rifts and over
> strawberry and artichoke fields, its bottomless mind
> returning always to the same rocks, the same cliffs, with
> ever-changing words, always the same language
> —this is where I live now.

It is also generous. Through to its final section, the poem embodies its fundamental issue—"What homage will be paid to beauty / that insists on speaking truth, knows the two are not always the same, / beauty that won't deny, is itself an eye, will not rest under contemplation?"

The difficult relationship between beauty and truth continues into the book's second part. Children and adults oppressed by war, poverty, racism, and moral failures are represented by language that expertly moves its emotional tones. One of the book's most heart-rending poems, "Tattered Kaddish," is spoken on behalf of "all suicides":

> Praise to life though ones we knew and loved
> loved it badly, too well, and not enough
>
>> Praise to life though it tightened like a knot
>> on the hearts of ones we thought we knew loved us

Each poem presents "the great question" asked by the "philosopher of oppression, theorist / of the victories of force," Simone Weil, *"What are you going through?"*—purposely speaking "from the marrow of our bones." The last poem, "Final Notations"— a kind of epilogue—could also be the book's prologue. The poem's two pronouns, "it" and "you," overlap, explode, and include the multitude of ideas, thoughts, and realities that people the book—but you have to read both pronouns, first of all, as representing the act of poetry itself, that which most forcefully opens up for us the depths of the difficult world: "it will not be simple, it will not be long"; "It will take all your flesh, it will not be simple"; "you are taking parts of us into places never planned / you are going far away with pieces of our lives"; "it will be short, it will take all your breath / it will not be simple, it will become your will."

It will not be simple, it will become your will: It is what makes both *An Atlas of the Difficult World* and *Flow Chart*—so different in their particular strategies—so very important. Each book brilliantly renews the critical act of creating poetry out of the tremendous reality of our lives. Taking in and giving back an intensified feeling for the worlds in which we live—conceiving language inside its most pressured verbal form—both books truly and deeply express what it is to write poetry in an overwhelmingly complex and common, difficult time.

Poets on Poets and Poetry

Wallace Stevens, in his 1951 introduction to *The Necessary Angel: Essays on Reality and the Imagination,* writes: "One function of the poet at any time is to discover by his own thought and feeling what seems to him to be the poetry at that time."

Eugenio Montale, in "Dante, Yesterday and Today," translated by Jonathan Galassi: "Always, at all times, poets have spoken to poets, entering into a real or imaginary correspondence with them."

Poetry, Elizabeth Bishop writes in a letter to May Swenson— quoted in *Edgar Allen Poe & the Juke-Box: Uncollected Poems, Drafts and Fragments*—is "a way of thinking with one's feelings."

Gottfried Benn, in "Double Life: Future and Present," translated by E. B. Ashton: "It is amazing . . . there is nothing more revealing than the word. It has always fascinated me to see experts in their fields, even profound philosophers, suddenly faced with the free word—the word that yields no tirades, no systems, no facts of external, historically buttressed observation, and no commentaries; that produces only one thing: form. How they operate there! Utterly at a loss. . . . Addendum: there really are now only two verbal transcendencies, the theorems of mathematics and the word as art."

Allen Ginsberg, in "Mind Writing Slogans": "Ordinary mind includes eternal perceptions. . . . Notice what you notice. . . . Catch yourself thinking. . . . Intense fragments of spoken idiom, best. . . . Subject is known by what she sees."

Jonathan Galassi, in "Reading Montale," in his book of translations of Eugenio Montale's *Collected Poems: 1920–1954*: "As Gian-
franco Contini has observed, Montale's work is written at the
point of 'veritable cultural saturation'; it is so heavily layered
with allusion and quotation, particularly self-quotation, that at
times it seems to approximate the echo chamber of Walter Benjamin's ideal work, the collage of borrowings."

James Schuyler's
The Morning of the Poem

I

James Schuyler's *The Morning of the Poem* was published in 1980 and received the Pulitzer Prize for that year. Like all Schuyler's poetry, *The Morning of the Poem* involves continuous experiments of language and form. If I had to choose a book that most reflects the staying-power of Schuyler's work, it would be (though the decision is a difficult one to make) *The Morning of the Poem*, which still, years after its publication, remains, in its entirety, alive and compelling, its surprises wondrous and endless.

II

In a few lines toward the end of "Dining Out With Doug and Frank"—a four-part poem that concludes *The Morning of the Poem*'s first section—the poet says,

> Through dinner
> I wanted to talk more than we
> did about Frank's poems. All it
> came down to was "experiment
> more," "try collages," and "write
> some skinny poems."

—one of many passages in *The Morning of the Poem* that presents the making of the poem as a dominant subject. A poet should be experimental. A poet should be modernist. Schuyler's poetry is both. Although every poem he writes is spoken by a particular, subjective self, Schuyler's "I" is, at the same time, revealed as con-substantial and coextensive with the poem itself. The writing subject is not only dependent on language, but is also part of it, placed in the position of questioning its own, and its language's, status and function. The language of a Schuyler poem exists on (at least) two separate yet overlapping planes: one where language is used as a medium of communicating meaning; the other, an aesthetic plane, where the language of the poem embodying the speaker-self possesses an autonomous value. "Try collages," the poet says—and does. Schuyler's poetry—like collage—demonstrates a sharp demarcation between the imagination and actual, everyday life. The real world is engulfed in an aesthetic venture: Each poem demands that it be looked at as a discovered object, a form of representational design that intensifies our sense of the medium itself. Schuyler's poetry seeks to achieve what Eugenio Montale in one of his essays on modernist poetry called (the translation is Jonathan Galassi's) "poetic-painterly musical production." The purpose of poetry, and the language of poetry, is "toward the object, toward art invested, incarnated in the means of expression, toward emotion which has become *thing*." "Understand here"—Montale continues— "that by thing we don't mean the external metaphor, the description, but simply the resistance of the word within its syntactical nexus, the objective, finished, and not at all Parnassian sense of form *sui generis,* to be judged case by case." For Montale and for Schuyler, too, the production of a poem—its creation into an object of projected subjective emotion—defines, in the first instance, what a poem is about.

A complex aesthetic, not easily reducible to critical restatement: You have to look at the poetry itself to see how it plays out. For example, the opening first sentence of the sixty-page title poem:

> July 8 or July 9 the eighth surely, certainly
>   1976 that I know
> Awakening in western New York blurred barely
>   morning sopping dawn
> Globules face to my face, a beautiful face, not
>   mine: Baudelaire's skull:

Force, fate, will, and, you being you: a
        painter, you drink
Your Ovaltine and climb to the city roof, "to
        find a view," and
I being whoever I am get out of bed holding
        my cock and go to piss
Then to the kitchen to make coffee and toast
        with jam and see out
The window two blue jays ripping something white
        while from my mother's
Room the radio purls: it plays all night she leaves
        it on to hear
The midnight news then sleeps and dozes
        until day which now it is,
Wakening today in green more gray, why did
        your lithe blondness
In Remsen handsomeness mix in my mind with
        Baudelaire's skull?

The intersecting syntactical combinations; corresponding shifts
in subject matter; the use (or lack) of punctuation to delineate
transitions of meaning and language; the sensually direct texture
of the talk; the fragmentation of the spoken-to "you"; the back
and forth, background and foreground, image-frames; the sense
of improvised lineation: What is undeniable is the subtle force by
which the poem's language is projected into form, into an object
of felt expression. Call it collage; call it projected verse; call it in-
scape: What you actually see, hear and feel, at its core, is the form
and language of the poem itself, what it perceptually embodies.

III

About three hundred lines into the title poem, Schuyler unexpectedly switches its shape and tone, returning to one of his
central subjects, poetry itself:

                So many lousy poets
                So few good ones
                What's the problem?
                No innate love of

Words, no sense of
How the thing said
Is in the words, how
The words are themselves
The thing said: love,
Mistake, promise, auto
Crack-up, color, petal,
The color in the petal
Is merely light
And that's refraction:
A word, that's the poem.

A remarkable passage (even out of context. In the flow of
the poem, its impact is even stronger). The problem with bad
poetry—no innate love of words, no sense of how the thing said
is in the words and the words are the thing said. Then, a series
of intuitively associative words that come at you contrapuntally,
compressed by what appear to be disparate meanings. "Love"
and "mistake" and "promise" are set immediately before "auto
crack-up"—in a book that earlier talks about "wham / a ner-
vous breakdown" and has a whole section, eleven "The Payne
Whitney Poems," which reference "in and out of mental / hos-
pitals"—followed by "color" and "petal"—which are then re-
opened into a sentence, "The color in the petal / Is merely
light /And that's refraction: / a word, that's the poem." "And
that's refraction"—and yet, it isn't clear what the "that's" refers
to . . . the light? the color in the petal that is merely light? the series of associative words? the preceding passage? Then, "A word,
that's the poem"—but what word? . . . words themselves? . . . and
what poem? this poem? every poem?

Read it again and this much is clear: Schuyler's poetry is
premised on refraction. The word's meaning from physics is the
breaking of the course of a substance (for example, light) into
another course, the deflection at a certain angle at the point of
passage from one medium of density into another. (In the six-
teenth century it meant "the act of breaking open, or breaking
up.") When applied to poetry, refraction describes the complex
variational processes involved in the creation of verbal music.
Spoken language, looked at musically, is a medium of changing
tones—vocal variations that reflect different densities of sound.

In the first instance, refracted language creates a formal aura that makes a poem—in Montale's terms—an object of musical production. A poet has to love words themselves—how they sound, how they are spoken, how, in a poem, they are formed at their most elementary level. Poems are constructed out of refractory verbal play (a process Schuyler metaphorically equates with light) made into junctures, or structures, of syntax and meaning: word, phrase, line, half-sentence, sentence, the poem itself.

In *The Morning of the Poem,* Schuyler openly probes his love of tonally refracted language. Some forty pages into the title poem, in the context of talking about a high school teacher who taught him poetry, the poet tells us:

> . . . Mr Smeltzer, who opened windows for me on
> flowering fields and bays where the water greenly danced,
> Knifed into waves by wind: the day he disclosed William Carlos
> Williams to us, writing a short and seemingly
> Senseless poem on the blackboard—I've searched the collected
> poems and am never sure which it is (Wallace
> Stevens, Marianne Moore, Elizabeth Bishop, I found for myself . . .

Williams, Stevens, Moore, Bishop: What the work of each has in common is the desire to create an aesthetic of rhetoric and of speech. Robert Lowell, in writing about Williams, observed that Williams's "idiom comes from many sources, from speech and reading, both of various kinds; the blend, which is his own invention, is generous and even exotic." What Lowell says about Williams also applies to Stevens, Moore, Bishop—and Schuyler too. Lowell relates how he once typed out a Williams poem, "The Semblables," into a single prose paragraph. Although "not a word or its placing has been changed," the poem "changed into a piece of smothering, magnificent rhetoric, much more like Faulkner than the original Williams." If you run the exercise through a Schuyler poem—for example, the densely spoken and observed "Dec. 28, 1974"—this is what you have:

> The plants against the light which shines in (it's four o'clock)
> right on my chair: I'm in my chair: are silhouettes, barely
> green, growing black as my eyes move right, right to where

the sun is. I am blinded by a fiery circle: I can't see what I write. A man comes down the iron stairs (I don't look up) and picks up brushes which, against a sonata of Scriabin's, rattle like wind in a bamboo clump. A wooden sound, and purposeful footsteps softened by a drop-cloth covered floor. To be encubed in flaming splendor, one foot on a Chinese rug, while the mad emotive music tears at my heart. Rip it open: I want to cleanse it in an icy wind. And what kind of tripe is that? Still, last night I *did* wish—no, that's my business and I won't wish it now. "Your poems," a clunkhead said, "have grown more open." I don't want to be open, merely to say, to see and say, things as they are. That at my elbow there is a wicker table. *Hortus Second* says a book. The fields beyond the feeding sparrows are brown, paley brown yet with an inward glow like that of someone of a frank good nature whom you trust. I want to hear the music hanging in the air and drink my Coca-Cola. The sun is off me now, the sky begins to color up, the air in here is filled with wildly flying notes. Yes, the sun moves off to the right and prepares to sink, setting, beyond the dunes, an ocean on fire.

Words jostle words (and the creation of words: for example, "encubed" and "paley"); subject matter is revealed by and through sped-up idiomatic, syntactic switches that twist the sentences out of their usual meanings. Sudden, reflective references are made to the act of writing itself: "I don't want to be open, / merely to say, to see and say, things / as they are" (which plays on Stevens's refrain about "things as they are" in "The Man with the Blue Guitar," revising it to encompass an aesthetic that "merely" sees and says).

Written out with Schuyler's chosen lineation, the language sounds nothing like what we think of as narrative prose:

> The plants against the light
> which shines in (it's four o'clock)
> right on my chair: I'm in my chair:
> are silhouettes, barely green,
> growing black as my eyes move right,
> right to where the sun is.
> I am blinded by a fiery circle:
> I can't see what I write. A man

comes down the iron stairs (I
don't look up) and picks up brushes
which, against a sonata of Scriabin's
rattle like wind in a bamboo clump.
A wooden sound, and purposeful footsteps
softened by a drop-cloth covered floor.
To be encubed in flaming splendor
one foot on a Chinese rug, while
the made emotive music
tears at my heart. Rip it open:
I want to cleanse it in an icy wind.
And what kind of tripe is that?
Still, last night I did wish—
no that's my business and I
won't wish it now. "Your poems,"
a clunkhead said, "have grown
more open." I don't want to be open,
merely to say, to see and say, things
as they are. That at my elbow
there is a wicker table. *Hortus
Second* says a book. The fields
beyond the feeding sparrows are
brown, paley brown yet with an inward glow
like that of someone of a frank good nature
whom you trust. I want to hear the music
hanging in the air and drink my
Coca-Cola. The sun is off me now,
the sky begins to color up, the air
here is filled with wildly flying notes.
Yes, the sun moves off to the right
and prepares to sink, setting,
beyond the dunes, and ocean on fire.

The lineation speeds, slows, simplifies, and condenses—*forms*—
the language's ornate syntactical structures, bringing the musical qualities of the vocal and perceptual shifts to the formal forefront, communicating another level of meaning in addition to the highly refracted conversational talk immediately at the surface. Note, also, how the lineation compresses the language and generates new meanings, demonstrating that the ultimate comprehension of the poem is in the poem itself. The

poem's projection of itself as an object of formed emotions demands that it be left alone and respected on its own terms, to be reread and reinterpreted over and over again.

IV

And Schuyler's subject matter? It is, of course, bound by his experiments of form and language. The immanent, variational, improvisational qualities of the poems—even the way that they're shaped visually on the page—determine not only how their subjects appear, but also what the poems are essentially about: the poet's thoughts of the day or even the moment, and the ongoing, seemingly instantaneous inward and outward perceptions of one who writes poetry. For Schuyler, the language of a poem proceeds by exploring whatever arises in the poet's mind and his or her daily life, and takes its shape from that. The particulars of a poem are connected to each other by the internal workings of the poem itself: The poem creates a state of mind capable of assimilating any and all thoughts, ideas, and perceptions into its own imaginative unities. The poet, like the dreamer, transforms choice into necessity, giving what appear to be randomly chosen materials specific locations within a system of relationships grounded on vision. Listen, for instance, to the last of Schuyler's eleven "The Payne Whitney Poems," the haunting "What":

> What's in those pills?
> After lunch and I can
> hardly keep my eyes
> open. Oh, for someone to
> talk small talk with.
> Even a dog would do.
>
> Why are they hammering
> iron outside? And what
> is that generator whose
> fierce hum comes in
> the window? What is a
> poem, anyway.

> The daffodils, the heather
> and the freesias all
> speak to me. I speak
> back, like St. Francis
> and the wolf of Gubbio.

A Schuyler poem is always intricately conversing: The poems are forms of talk intended for and directed toward an actual "you." (What Louis Zukofsky wrote applies to Schuyler's poetry, too: "Talk is a form of love / let us talk.") Schuyler obsessively explores the musical possibilities of ordinary talk about ordinary people and things. The poems never lose their communicative impulse, which makes them profoundly human, ultimately driven by a love of, and desire for, intricate expression. This all-too-human spoken side of Schuyler's language constantly measures his aesthetic. And, as far as Schuyler explores form and language—and he does so profoundly—the results are (I use the word carefully) great. His work reveals—as much as that of any American poet this century—that form, not content, is what first of all creates immediacy, intensity, and depth, that the language of a poem provides the threshold through which our need to touch reality is satisfied. The closer the language of a poem can get to reality, the deeper and truer the impression it will make on our common feelings.

V

The morning of Friday, April 12, 1991, James Schuyler died at the age of sixty-seven, after suffering a stroke a week before. According to the *New York Times,* there were "no immediate survivors."

The phrase reminded me of a later poem of Montale's, "To Conclude," in which he speaks to "my descendants (if I have any) on the literary plane."

James Schuyler's immediate survivors—his descendants—include whoever on the literary plane of American poetry writes poetry after him.

Word Made Flesh

I

It was May. The Jesuit high school in Detroit. The Gospel According to John.

"Love. God. Is. God *is* love. Do you understand?" Father Born asked. "Each word means the same thing. That's what God is. Love."

"Th*aaa*t's what love is m*aaaa*de of," Przywara whispered across the aisle, imitating the voice of Smokey Robinson.

"In the beginning is the word. The word is with God. The word is God and God is love. That," Born said, "is what this Gospel is about. There's a prophet—John the Baptist is a prophet. A voice crying—howling, screaming, shouting, crying. A witness—*Ut testimonium perhiberet de lumine.* One who provides testimony. Testimony as to what? To what is seen. And what is seen? Light. And what is light? The word. And what is the word? Made flesh. *Verbum caro factum est.* God is the word made alive among us. *Habitavit in nobis.* A part of us—a part of our lives. The incarnation of the word of God. This"—Born's voice suddenly turned intense—"this and the redemption of every human being by the sacrifice of a God of eternal love, fully God and fully human crucified on a cross, killed under the laws of the Roman state. These are the central mysteries of our faith. The central mysteries of our faith have to do with love. Then, now . . . right now . . . the word, God, love, among us, alive, right now . . . Right, Przywara?"

Przywara—pounding the song's beat out on his desk with flattened palms, loud enough for the whole room to hear, his head shaking back and forth—was singing Marvin Gaye's "Can I Get a Witness."

"Right, Przywara? Even you can see what I mean, can't you? Basic logic. God is love, God is the word made flesh . . . so therefore . . ."

"God is love in the flesh," Przywara answered. Everyone laughed. "No, really," Przywara said. "What you were saying. All this about God and love and the word. Sort of abstract, isn't it? But what does it really *mean*?"

Born was surprised by the question. He paused an instant and then smiled. "Well, that is *the* question, Przywara. Good. We'll leave it at that. Enough for the day. This word business— well, it's serious stuff."

"It *is* serious," Przywara said after class. "I mean, what if it all *is* words. That words are what we are. That what we do is what we say. Do-be-do-be"—he started to laugh—"now what I s*aaaaa*y. No"—he paused—"seriously. What if what we say—how we say it, why we say it, when we say it—*is* what *is*. What love"—he moaned the word the way that Smokey would—"*iiiiiiii*s. Think about that"—his voice was mimicking Lyndon Johnson's— "m*aaa*h fell*ooo*w Am*aaa*ricans. Think about it. God is, love is, words. Our words, right here, right now, in D*eee*troit city, this, the year of Our Lord nineteen hundred and sixty-six . . ." Przywara stopped. He shook his head several times, then smiled again. "Fuck. F*uuuuuu*ck. The whole thing sort of boggles the fucking human mind, now doesn't it?"

II

But, after all, that city, Detroit, was, at that time, a serious place. Millions who had come there during this century to work. A large working class and an industrialist class among the wealthiest in the world. Parts of the city sectioned into massive factory complexes. An inner city in which the poor lived. A city of churches and a city of bars. Avenues named Grand River and Jefferson, Gratiot and Woodward. Ford and Chrysler expressways. Street after street lined with oaks, elms, catalpas, silver and red maples. A river—actually a strait between two Great Lakes (in winter often dark green with ice floes)—bordered on one side by Canada. In the strait, a municipal park, Belle Isle (designed by

Frederick Olmstead), with woods and deer. A city, you might say, strategically located to the Pittsburgh-Youngstown steel mills, the Akron rubber plants, the Messabi iron range, to the Great Lakes waterways . . .

America's most violent city was Detroit. The nation was at war. My generation was being conscripted, mostly those of the lower middle class or poor. The streets changed fast; guns could be bought for almost nothing and were used, often by those who returned from Indo-China knowing how to kill if they had to, many of them addicted to heroin, and unemployed, while, inflated by war, the economy boomed. I was nineteen in late July, nineteen sixty-seven, when the city was set on fire. An insurrection the magnitude of which no one could have imagined. I saw it. My father's and uncle's small grocery and liquor store was looted and burned. Divisions of the armed forces dispatched by the president. I'd just completed my first year of college. That summer I worked afternoon shift in a factory in Pontiac, at General Motors Truck & Coach, dry-sanding bodies of Chevrolet vans as they came out of a primer oven.

Language turned physical. All sorts of languages, including those of the Catholic Bible I had known since childhood. From the beginning of the Book of Genesis, the repetition of the words "and God said let there be"—God's words on fire, appearing before the prophet Moses, the word of God among the prophets Isaiah and Jeremiah, Ezekiel, Daniel, Micah, and Amos eight, seven, centuries before Christ—the word of God witnessed in books that address the deepest human troubles through heightened, hyper-conscious, spoken language.

Two or so years later, I discovered, in the opening words of the Book of Jeremiah (the translation is mine, composed from several different translations):

> Now the word of the God came to me saying, "Before I formed you in the womb, I knew you, before you were born I consecrated you, I appointed you as a prophet to the nations" . . . I said, "My God, I do not know how to speak, I am only a child." But God replied, "Do not say, 'I am only a child.' Go now to those whom I send you and say whatever I command you." Then God put his hand out and touched my mouth and said,

"There! I have put my words in your mouth . . . See, I have, today, set you over nations and over kingdoms, to root out, and to pull down, to destroy, and to throw down, to build, and to plant."

A month or so after that—shortly after my father was shot during a robbery in his store, "the poor man was so hopped-up on heroin," he said later of the man who shot him, "he didn't even know the gun went off"—I wrote:

> I was appointed the poet of heaven.
>
> It was my duty to describe
> Theresa's small roses
> as they bent in the wind.
>
> I tired of this
> and asked you to let me
> write about something else.
> You ordered, "Sit
> in the trees where the angels sleep
> and copy their breaths
> in verse."
>
> So I did,
> and soon I had a public following:
>
> Saint Agnes with red cheeks,
> Saint Dorothy with a moon between her fingers
> and the Hosts of Heaven.
>
> You said, "You've failed me."
> I told you, "I'll write lovelier poems,"
> but, you answered,
> "You've already had your chance:
>
> you will be pulled from a womb
> into a city."

III

"'Theology after breakfast sticks to the eye,'" a friend said, quoting Wallace Stevens's poem "Les Plus Belles Pages," laughing after I told him that I'd been thinking a lot lately about the theology of the word. "The theology of the word? Take a look," he said, "at Paul's epistles to the Corinthians."

I'd never read either of them all the way through. An epistle—a classical form, speaking in writing to another, or to others about common issues. Paragraph after paragraph written against the "wicked" in the city of Corinth are interspersed throughout both epistles: "Whatever you eat, whatever you drink, whatever you do at all, do it for the glory of God." But the prescriptive side of the language isn't what holds your attention: What you first of all feel is the illumination of good and evil by an openly changing intensity of expression—the writer's (even if it is the translator's or the writer's translation of the translator's) voice. Suddenly, for example, in the second epistle—shortly after Paul says that his epistle isn't intended "to condemn," that the Corinthians are "in our hearts"—Paul gives the following "suggestion":

> A man is acceptable for whatever he has, not for what he does not have. This does not mean that to give relief to others you ought to make things difficult for yourselves: It is a question of balancing what happens to be your abundance now against what they need now; one day they may have something to spare that you may need. As it is written, "He who gathered much had none too much, he who gathered little was not lacking."

A few pages later, after the writer boasts about his authority, we hear him say, almost apologetically, "I am speaking as a fool . . . I am talking like a madman." Then, near the end of the epistle, the tone is changed again: "I warned those who sinned before and all the others, and I warn them now while absent . . . that if I come again I will not spare them." There's also talk about the meaning of talk itself. The distinction is made between speaking in tongues and prophecy: "He who speaks in an unknown tongue edifies himself. . . . But he who prophesies speaks to others, to edification, and exhortation, and comfort." The holiest language takes account of others; it has to do with the world.

And for Paul of Tarsus—versed in the prophets, blinded and rendered speechless "when a light from heaven flashed around him" (God's voice speaking to him outside his will, telling him he would be told what to do, so transformed by the experience that his very name was changed)—there is his testimony, toward the end of the first epistle to the Corinthians, to this:

> If I speak in the tongues of men and of angels, but speak without love, I am simply a noisy gong or a clashing cymbal. And if I have the powers of prophecy, and understand all the mysteries there are, and know everything, and even have the faith to move mountains, without love I am nothing. If I give away all that I have but am without love, I am no good whatsoever. Love never ends. The powers of prophecy will pass away; the gift of tongues will cease to be; and knowledge—it, too, one day will pass away. For our knowledge is imperfect, and our prophecy is imperfect, but once perfection comes all imperfect things will disappear . . . For now we see through a glass darkly, but then we will see face to face. Now I know in part, then I will know as fully as I am known . . . So there are three things that last, faith, hope and love, but the greatest of these is love.

. . . words that I heard for the first time as a child, during that part of the Ordinary of the Mass when the priest reads a passage from Scripture, the common prayer called the Epistle.

IV

So on this past Feast of the Incarnation I reflected on the word made flesh. A chilly wind slid through the green and blue morning air. I walked down to Battery Park. The harbor blazed with light. A woman and a man on the esplanade were talking animatedly to one another, the words between them dissolving in the watery light. A man wrapped in blankets was talking out loud to himself.

Not far from Coenties Slip and Water Street—a few blocks from Wall Street—there is a war memorial. Words of soldiers etched into a green glass wall:

20 Apr 70

Dear Gail,

You don't know how close I have been to getting killed
or maimed. Too many times I have seen guys near me get
hit and go home in a plastic bag . . . It is time to forget.
But it's hard to forget these things. I close my eyes and
try to sleep but all I can see is Jenkins laying there with
his brains hanging out or Lefty with his eyes shot out . . .
Then you stop to think, it could be me. Hell, I don't
know why I'm writing all this. But it feels better getting it
out of my mind. I love you, Pete

SP *1* 4 Peter H. Roepke
A *3/506* Inf.
I 0 I st Airborne Div.
Thua Thieu

On a pier on the East River I look in my notebook at these
words of a poet: "Sometimes the 'you' is me, talking with myself.
Other times 'you' is someone else I'm talking to, even the 'you'
who created me. Other times it could be 'you' talking with 'you.'
The 'I' also changes. It could be me, it could be someone else.
And, when I say 'he,' sometimes I mean me." I read: "Catholic.
The Catholic. Being Catholic . . . William Carlos Williams: the
Pere Sebastian Rasles chapter in *In the American Grain*. Written in
the context of a Puritan, Protestant America in the early twenties. 'Rasles . . . A Catholic, a Jesuit . . . To mystery rightly rea-
soned, logic is consigned . . . It is *this* to be *moral*: to be *positive*,
to be peculiar, to be sure, generous brave—to MARRY, to
touch—to give because one HAS and to give to him who HAS,
who will join, who will make to create, not to sterilize, to dry
up, to rot . . . And so America is become the greatest ground
for the Catholics in the world today—in spite of everything . . .
a field where tenderness may move, love may awaken and a way
if offered.' Flannery O'Connor—her desire, as a Catholic, 'to
penetrate the surface of reality . . . to find in each thing the
spirit that makes itself, to hold the world together.' Merleau-
Ponty. The incarnation changes everything. After the incarnation, God is externalized, is seen in a certain historical place at

a certain historical time. The incarnated God leaves behind words and memories that are then passed on. After the incarnation, the human journey toward God is no longer achieved solely by contemplation, but also through the commentary on, and interpretation of, written texts—texts whose energy is never exhausted, written stories that open and reopen the question of the distinction between body and spirit, between interior and exterior. The word becoming flesh means that the truths of God are found in and through human beings. The form of the Gospel stories is in the stories' metaphorical content. The Gospel's stories do not invoke the idea of God, but are the vehicle of God's presence and action."

Later that day, I look again at the Book of Jeremiah: "For this word is like fire, like a hammer that breaks the rocks into pieces," and yet, "I found your words and your word was the joy and rejoicing of my heart." Through words he is taken into God's indignation, love, sorrow. Nothing to do with a sense of doom, but with a sense of judgment. The prophet doubts (as God, too, really doubts) what to do, how to do it. Detached not only from his own likes or dislikes, but from God, too, with whom he quarrels, speaking for those who have to live in, not make, history, his emotions collective, sublimated, and ironic, revealing those truths that struggle for expression in our hearts, sometimes in a code of which we take in only as much as we can.

"The language of the prophets? It's not that complicated," one of the people in this world I'm closest to said when I told her what I'd been thinking. "If you have to rethink the whole situation—which some of us seem chronically compelled to do—you need to imagine a language to do it, don't you? That's what those books are about. Have you ever read Isaiah chapter by chapter? It's a book of poems. Light and more light. The sharper the light is, the more glaring the distortions the writer sees around him. The sense of the body charged with words—God-words, human words. The feeling of language making something new, or, at least, words made as intense as existence. Language sparked, transposed, transformed—creating. In that sense divine.

"Think of it," she went on, "think what 'In the beginning was the word' really means. Among the Jews were these strange moralists who knew, through this ongoing conversation in writing with one another, that the universe is revealed through words. The whole thing. Everything. Think of it. Biologically, we're pure emotion but, alone among the animals, we're given words. The result? The politician. The writer. And those Jewish prophets—and, if I remember right, in Catholic theology, Christ is the last among them—understood what this meant. The pressures of the word are overwhelming. To use words you don't hear much anymore—awe-inspiring. Like the feeling of life itself."

I go back to the Gospel of John. I'd forgotten how it ended. "And there are also many other things that Jesus did, and, if all of them were written, there wouldn't be enough space in the entire world to contain all the books necessary to tell about them." The final verse of the final Gospel. A book beginning "In the beginning was the word, and the word was with God, and the word was God" ending in words that say no words can express the life of one person. A repeated sending-forth of words—God made alive by the transmission of his life into words, making its way into history, never-ending. . . .

"Listen," she insisted. "Just listen!"

"All right," I said. "All right, I'll listen."

"She was propped up in her bed in this—God, I can't even say the word. Home. We call them homes! A dwelling! Her hair white and wild, her body unable to move of its own accord. Then, suddenly, she began to . . . you couldn't really call it talk. I wiped her lips, they were parched from the medication. She began to . . . what's the word? What she was doing was making sounds. But she was looking right at me. She was *conversing. Communicating.* Suddenly, she began to sing, a kind of guttural chant, a song, I think, from her childhood. She was able to form only a few words I understood. 'You.' 'I.' 'Remember.' But it was mostly those sounds—intonations you might call them—from deep inside her—God, this woman who spoke so beautifully, who taught me my words. There she was, as alive as I'd ever known her, trying to say what she was feeling. There we were. And do you know what I think? There is no such thing as no language. Because that's what it was—language. What we say, what we don't say, what can be expressed, what can't be . . ."

"I don't understand. You mean that she . . ."

"She went on like that for almost an hour. A woman, much older, badly crippled, in the bed next to hers kept saying, 'She's talking! She's talking! It's a miracle! She's talking!' The more she got into those sounds—her eyes widened until they were almost transparent, they had color again, they'd changed from dark brown, almost black, to gray and green . . ."

"Her eyes changed color?"

"Yes. While I was there. Her eyes actually changed color! There she was—God, what a beautiful woman!—raising her voice, lowering it, trying to move her body, singing again, her face softening, her head slightly nodding up and down, tilting sideways. Then, suddenly, she closed her eyes, and never spoke to me again."

A Few Reflections on
Poetry and Language

I

In "When Was Modernism?"—which appeared in *New Left Review* in 1989—Raymond Williams defined what modernism is by asking when it was. As a classification for a whole cultural movement and moment, "modernism"—Williams pointed out—did not appear until the 1950s; until then, the meaning of "modern" in literature was roughly the same as "contemporary." Modernism is, therefore, a critical construct; modernist writers "are applauded for their denaturalizing of language, their break with the allegedly prior view that language is either a clear, transparent glass or a mirror, and for their making abruptly apparent in the texture of narrative the problematic status of the author and his authority." As the author appears in the text, the "self-reflexive text assumes the centre of the public and aesthetic stage, and in doing so declaratively repudiates the fixed forms."

Or, as Peter Burger writes in an essay, "Aporias of Modern Aesthetics"—published in *New Left Review* a year after "When Was Modernism"—after modernism "art is itself dragged into the process of alienation that separates subject and object." In the context of a crisis first imagined by Nietzsche, the romantic writer's belief in the self's power to shape reality through language, and the realist's sense of language as an accurate expression of factitious reality, are shattered. Modernist writing—as Charles Taylor observes in *Sources of the Self*—turns more inward, tending to explore, even to celebrate, subjectivity, exploring "new recesses of feeling," entering the "stream of consciousness," spawning "schools of art rightly 'expressionist,' while, at the same time, decentering the subject," displacing "the center of interest onto language, or onto poetic transmutation itself, or even dissolving the self as usually conceived in favor of some new constellation." The paradox, aesthetically, is this: Although the subject is dissolved into the text's language—into the formal process itself, onto a new and separate aesthetic plane—modernism does not eliminate subjectivity.

In "Subjective Authenticity"—a 1976 interview with Hans Kaufmann—Christa Wolf says that the "reservoir writers draw on in their writing is experience, which mediates between objective reality and the authorial subject." Quoting Anna Seghers, who said that the writer "is the curious crossing point where object becomes subject and turns back into object," Wolf continues in a passage worth quoting at length:

> To my mind it is much more useful to look at writing, not as an end product, but as a process which continuously runs *alongside life,* helping to shape and interpret it: writing can be seen as a way of being more intensely involved in the world, as the concentration and focusing of thought, word and deed. This mode of writing is not "subjectivist," but "interventionist." It does require subjectivity, and a subject who is prepared to undergo unrelenting exposure—that is easy to say, of course, but I really do mean as unrelenting as possible—to the material at hand, to accept the burden of the tensions that inexorably arise, and to be curious about the changes that both material and the author undergo. The new reality you see is different from the one you saw before. Suddenly, everything is interconnected and fluid. Things formerly taken as "given" start to dissolve, revealing the reified social relations they contain and no longer that hierarchically arranged social cosmos in which the human particle travels along the paths pre-ordained by sociology or ideology, or deviates from them. It becomes more and more difficult to say "I," and yet at the same time often imperative to do so. I can only hope I have made it clear that this method not only does not dispute the existence of objective reality, but is precisely an attempt to engage with "objective reality" in a productive manner.

II

Theories of language appear throughout modernist poetics. As Sigurd Burckhardt noted in his still worth reading 1956 essay "The Poet as Fool and Priest," the "first purpose of poetic language is the very opposite of making language more transparent." If a language pure enough to transmit human experience without distortion existed, there would be no need for poetry. Not only does such a language not exist, it cannot; language, by its very nature, is as a social instrument, and must be a convention, arbitrarily ordering the chaos of experiences, denying expression to some, allowing it to others. Language must provide common denominators, and so it necessarily falsifies. These falsifications are more dangerous the more transparent language becomes—the more unquestioningly it is accepted as an undistorting medium. Language itself—as Michael Hamburger puts it his 1969 critical magnum opus, *The Truth of Poetry: Tensions in Modern Poetry from Baudelaire to the 1960s*—"guarantees that no poetry will be totally 'dehumanized,' regardless whether a poet attempts to project pure inwardness outwards or to lose and find himself in animals, plants and inanimate things." Words never can be totally severed from the ideas and meanings that exist in external reality. One needn't be a Marxist to recognize that all poetry has political, social and moral implications, regardless whether the intention behind it is didactic and "activist" or not.

Poets, always the most astute theoreticians and critics of their art, recognized the complicated refraction of the self in a poem by the early 1920s. "Poetry," William Carlos Williams writes in 1923 in *Spring and All*, expresses "new form dealt with as a reality in itself," the "dynamization of emotion into a separate form." Take, for example, Marianne Moore's "When I Buy Pictures," in her book *Observations*, published in 1924:

When I Buy Pictures

or what is closer to the truth,
when I look at that of which I may regard myself as the
    imaginary possessor,
I fix upon what would give me pleasure in my average
    moments:

the satire upon curiosity in which no more is discernible
than the intensity of the mood;
or quite the opposite—the old thing, the mediaeval
    decorated hat-box,
in which there are hounds with waists diminishing like the
    waist of the hour-glass,
and deer and birds and seated people;
it may be no more than a square of parquetry; the literal
    biography perhaps,
in letters standing well apart upon a parchment-like
    expanse;
an artichoke in six varieties of blue; the snipe-legged
    hieroglyphic in three parts;
the silver fence protracting Adam's grave, or Michael taking
    Adam by the wrist.
Too stern an intellectual emphasis upon this quality or that
    detracts from one's enjoyment.
It must not wish to disarm anything; nor may the approved
    triumph easily be honoured—
that which is great because something else is small.
It comes to this: of whatever sort it is,
it must be "lit with piercing glances into the life of things";
it must acknowledge the spiritual forces which have made it.

Note how Moore immediately decenters the poem's self. The
simple opening declaration, "When I buy pictures," is transformed into a more complicated statement, "when I look at that
of which I may regard myself as the imaginary possessor," which
the self sees as "closer to the truth." This long, dense line—
thickened by the accentuated jostling of its opening eight
monosyllables—enmeshes the "I" in its language. It also relo-
cates the "I" outside the self, in an aesthetic realm. Then, in a
long and complicated sentence—syntactically refracted by clo-
sures demarcated by a colon, a dash, and a series of semi-
colons—the "I" is fixed (in the sense of adjusted?) to the imagined object. The effect is to make the self doubly removed from
the actual act of buying, in a kind of perceptual reality that is no
more "than the intensity of the mood" or (continuing the
process of decentering) "quite the opposite—the old thing,"
which is first described, and then shifted back through layers of

meaning into subjectivity, "literal biography perhaps." At this point, the reader already has felt the poem as an imaginary object; the poem has assumed the center of attention and aesthetic focus, beyond "Too stern an intellectual quality." The imagined object—the picture turned into the poem—"must not wish to disarm anything." A poem includes wishes; it must be human; it cannot escape social or economic realities (those subtextually suggested by buying pictures, purchasing imagined enjoyment); it cannot ("perhaps") escape "literal biography." The poem in which the self chooses to imagine buying a picture "of whatever sort" has its own necessity. It must see "'into the life of things,'" yet must also "acknowledge" (a word connoting objectivity) its subjectivity, "the spiritual forces" which (both separate and part of it) make the poem what it must be. "Moore"—William Carlos Williams wrote in an essay on her poetry in 1925—"undertakes in her work to separate the poetry from the subject entirely—like all the moderns. In this she has been rarely successful and this is important. There is no compromise. Moore never falls from the place inhabited by poems. It is hard to give an illustration of this from her work because it is everywhere."

III

In part XXII of "The Man with the Blue Guitar"—written during the Great Depression (in 1935 or 1936), quite purposely with the title of the Pablo Picasso painting—Wallace Stvens writes: "Poetry is the subject of the poem, / From this the poem issues . . ." Or—to restate Stevens—every poem reflects what the poet believes poetry is; every poem composes its own poetics.

Stevens was the first American poet to make the issues of a poem his explicit subject. A poet's critical sense of a poem, of poetry, is reflected in the issues of the poet's poems. The subject matter of poetry is not that "collection of solid, static objects extended in space"—Stevens writes several years later, in his 1941 essay "The Noble Rider and the Sound of Words" (written after completing his book of poems *Parts of a World*—"but the life that is lived in the scene that it composes."

IV

One issue of poetry is a poem's existence as an object. As Octavio Paz writes in his essay, "Jose Ortega y Gasset: The Why and the Wherefore" (translated by Michael Schmidt): "The poem is a verbal object, and though it is made of signs (words), its ultimate reality unfolds beyond those signs: it is the presentation of a form." Paz echoes what Eugenio Montale in "Let's Talk about Hermeticism" (translated by Jonathan Galassi) wrote: That "the tendency" of a poem, "among all the infinite variations" is "toward the object, toward art invested, incarnated in the means of expression, toward emotion which has become *thing*," to be judged, formally, "case by case."

On Wednesday, March 21, 2006, in "Dispatches: Journals," a Poetry Foundation website and blog, Jonathan Galassi updates the issue. "I'm afraid"—Galassi writes—"I'm unavoidably wedded to the notion that a poem is a made thing that aims to be an autonomous object—a thing, with a life of its own . . . I guess I'm the learn-by-doing-type—poetics to me seem mainly ex post facto, derived from what one has already made out of what one has felt." On Thursday, March 23, 2006, Galassi writes: "I keep obsessing about my sense of a poem as a made thing—feeling kneaded and shaped into ideas, or is it conditioned by ideas, pressed through the mold of mental forms to become an autonomous object that somehow recapitulates the process? Or should we think of the poem as the process itself, the conversion of perception or emotion into . . . something? And how are those conversions determined by the history of the mind that's performing the transmutation—by what it's read and done before? . . . But what is poetry that isn't tied to a tradition, which is, after all what a language is?" On Friday, March 24, 2006—concluding his week of blogging—Galassi notes: "I went to see a performance of Mark Morris's company last week which included his version of the Gertrude Stein/Virgil Thompson opera, *Four Saints in Three Acts.* I was captivated again, as I always am, by the magic of Stein's words: 'pigeons on the grass, alas,' etc. Is she not the original 'language' poet? She unpacks syntax and expected meaning so constantly and surprisingly, with beautiful, witty, moving results" but "always works in reaction to expectation."

Terry Eagleton addresses the issue of the autonomy of the poem in a 1989 interview, "Action in the Present," in *Polygraph: Versions of the Present: Modernism / Postmodernism.* "There is a sense," Eagleton says, "that style in writing resists commodification, in a world where it is part of the effect of the commodity to desensualize. . . . I think we have to find a way to resist that form of commodification in the letter of the text . . . a way of resisting commodification by sensuousness, by a kind of . . . overlaying of the language."

V

In *A Novellette,* written in the late twenties, William Carlos Williams writes, "Conversation as design"; conversation expressed in a written text is, Williams says, "actual to the extent that it would be pure design . . . of which there is none in novels." Fifteen years or so later, T. S. Eliot, in "The Music of Poetry," writes: "It may be strange, that when I profess to be talking about the 'music' of poetry, I put such emphasis upon conversation. . . . While poetry attempts to convey something beyond what can be conveyed in prose rhythms, it remains, all the same, one person talking to another."

How does a poet converse in a poem? By "voices," Eliot says, in 1953, in "The Three Voices of Poetry." "The first voice is the voice of the poet talking to himself—or to nobody. The second," according to Eliot, "is the voice of the poet addressing an audience, whether large or small. The third is the voice of the poet when he attempts to create a dramatic character speaking in verse; when he is saying, not what he would say in his own person, but only what he can say within the limits of one imaginary character addressing another imaginary character. . . . I think"—Eliot concludes—"that in every poem, from the private meditation to the epic or the drama, there is more than one voice to be heard."

What is conveyed within the composition (or design) of a poem's voices beyond what can be conveyed in prose? Still the best answer to the question is Ezra Pound's declaration in 1934, in *ABC of Reading*: "'Great literature is simply language charged with meaning to the utmost possible degree' . . . I begin with poetry"—Pound writes—"because it is the most concentrated form of verbal expression."

Or—to restate Pound—poetry is all that language is, expressed in its most compressed, concentrated forms.

VI

The issue of a poem's language also creates issues of who the speaking (or conversing) self in a poem is. Michael Hamburger, in *The Truth of Poetry*'s "A Period Loose at All Ends" chapter, observes that in Eugenio Montale's poetry "private and public experiences are interwoven into the texture" of the poems "exactly as they are interwoven in the texture of human life." Montale's "poetic 'I' functions as a medium rather than as a subject (in either sense of the word)"; the poet "belongs to his poems, and his poems belong to any reader prepared to entrust himself to their exploratory courses." "The first person in a lyrical poem should never be identified, in any case, with the poet's empirical self," Hamburger writes in the *The Truth of Poetry*'s "Masks" chapter, discussing William Butler Yeats's poetry. Yeats, Hamburger says, "demands to be read with the kind of adjustments that we make for dramatic poetry. . . . Whether primarily confessional or primarily dramatic, the first person in lyrical poetry serves to convey a gesture, not to document identity or establish biographical facts." Yeats's "multiple selves . . . convey a great many different gestures, of a great many different orders."

In a 1982 review in *Stand* of Bertolt Brecht's *Poems 1913–1956,* Terry Eagleton writes that Brecht's aesthetic objective "was to float language free of the object so that it became not its mirror, but its critique." Language for Brecht was not a reflection or symbolic embodiment of reality, but a "historical intervention, shattering established representations in the name of alternative ways of constructing the world. The paradigm of such reconstructions for Brecht was"—Eagleton continues—"of course socialism, but there is a sense in which it was also writing. For any piece of writing constructs reality in partial, questionable, exclusive ways. The most revolutionary gesture for Brecht was for a poem to demonstrate its own bias, backtrack skeptically on its own assumptions, interrogate its own perceptions in the very act of communicating them." The political force of Brecht's poetry, therefore, "is not in the first place a question of 'passionate commitment,' moral indignation or satiric denunciation though few modern poets have equalled him in these capacities," but, instead, "a matter of dramatizing, in the very forms of fiction, that the social reality under which we live in merely one possibility, a particular 'fictional' construction which may be transformed. This"—Eagleton summarizes—"is indeed a question of form rather than (in the first place) of content, and it is for this reason that formalism must be opposed: it trivialises an issue of supreme importance."

Adrienne Rich, in the epigraph of her book *Telephone Ringing in the Labyrinth: Poems 2004–2006,* presents the issue simply like this: "Poetry is not self-expression, the I is a dramatic I," she writes, quoting Michael S. Harper, who quotes Sterling A. Brown.

VII

In the October 4, 2007, *Guardian,* John Freeman writes an article entitled "Verse-slinging." Freeman begins with an anecdote about stopping by "a Greenwich Village bookstore recently" where, on the store's front table, "a handsome batik-print covered paperback," *Contemporary American Poetry,* selected and introduced by Donald Hall, caught his eye. As he looked through what he thought looked like "a dignified little book," the bookseller—in a tone of voice Freeman describes "as if I were picking up a bullet casing"—interjected, "'Oh, the old poetry anthology wars . . . Now that was fun to watch from the sidelines.'"

"I hadn't stumbled on an old gunslinger, or a man drenched in nostalgia—just a bookseller with a long memory," Freeman continues. "During the 1950s and early 60s, what the Beats didn't accomplish in coffee houses and on City Lights Press, anthologists hammered home in the pages of pocket-sized books that sold for a dollar. They feel today like field manuals, complete with marshalling introductions. 'For thirty years'"—Freeman quotes from Hall's introduction to *Contemporary American Poetry*—"'an old orthodoxy ruled American poetry.'" American poetry, Hall wrote, has been "'derived from the orthodoxy of T.S. Eliot and the New Critics,'" who "'asked for a poetry of symmetry, intellect, irony, and wit. The last few years have broken the control of this orthodoxy.'"

Freeman doesn't elaborate on how the control of the orthodoxy that Hall mentions was critically broken. He simply observes that "It's hard to imagine this sentence being written today. It's not," Freeman says, "that there isn't an orthodoxy," but "rather that there are too many of them. There are lyric poets and language poets, slam poets and funny poets. There are poets who identify by ethnicity, gender, and sex," and—even among these—"many who could claim the mantle of such identity politics and refuse. But mostly, it should be said, there's a lot of poetry. . . . No longer do Americans have to read a prevailing kind of poetry, or even within their own borders."

Yet, Freeman asks, "in this mishmash" has something gotten lost? "What is a poem, anymore? Let alone a good one, or even a beautiful one? Who sets this taste? These," Freeman adds, "are not idle questions." In "an environment where poetry is as marginalised as it's ever been . . . despite the volume of stuff that's being produced," how do we "figure out what is good, and why it should matter," and then, how, do we "make those judgments heard?" when, today, "the taste-making power of anthologies has been replaced by MFA programs" and "a staggering proliferation of prizes."

VIII

So, what is a poem anymore (in an environment in which poetry is as marginalized as ever, and this marginalization is discussed and analyzed by poets more than the critical issues of the art itself)? The self-reflective text that assumes the center of the public and aesthetic stage; new form dealt with as a reality in itself; the most concentrated form of verbal expression, of composed vocal conversation; the notion of a made thing that aims to be an autonomous object, a *thing* with a life of its own, in which a life is lived in, in which a voice or voices function as a medium or as media, rather than as a subject or as subjects: "Poetry is the subject of the poem, / From this the poem issues." The issues of a poem are what a poem *is*.

In "Defying Conclusions: Opening Up Modernism," the final chapter of his 1995 book *Modernism in Poetry: Motivations, Structures and Limits,* Ranier Emig writes: "In order to fulfill itself, modernist poetry must keep a precarious balance. It must pursue modernity's tendency of transforming reality into an aesthetic construct. Yet it must not give in to a complete aestheticisation of reality, to the idea of its own omnipotence in the allure of its simulated reality. Self-reflection"—Emig says—"is the key term in modernist poetry's delicate balancing act. It must of necessity constitute itself and even strive to achieve an impossible unity. This is, as Adorno reminds us, the inheritance of myth as an attempt to master the chaos of nature."

Hayden Carruth

Hayden Carruth's *Collected Shorter Poems 1946–1991*—as the poet tells us in a prefatory note—includes about two-thirds of his published shorter poems, as well as a section "New Poems (1986–1991)." Written during a contentious period of American literary and political history, *Collected Shorter Poems 1946–1991* is monumental in its scope.

Carruth is a poet of ambition. Positioning himself within various American poetic traditions, he aggressively explores our times, our places, our language. Knowledge and reality become not only sources of poetic expression, but also objects of poetic desire: Carruth is never afraid to think about what is happening around him; he feels no imaginative discrepancy between thought and emotion, and he feels deeply. On one level, the poetry is personal, arising out of the responses of an actual self; on another level, the poet is always alert to American collective consciousness. Among the poets of his generation, Carruth—perhaps more than any other—has comprehended the profound aesthetic shifts in American modernist poetics. Take a look, for example (which I often do) at Carruth's 1970 anthology, *The Voice That Is Great Within Us: American Poetry of the Twentieth Century* (which is still very much in print). Carruth was the first poet anthologist to question post–World War II poetic orthodoxies, displaying, by example, the critical landscape of American poetry from Robert Frost (born in 1875) to Jim Harrison and Dianne Wakowski (both born in 1937). *The Voice That Is Great Within Us* (a title taken from Wallace Stevens) includes—among many other as aesthetically diverse poets—Mina Loy and Elinor Wylie, Charles Reznikoff and John Wheelwright, Langston Hughes and Lorine Niedecker, Theodore Roethke and Louis Zukofsky, Elizabeth Bishop and Charles Olson, Robert Hayden and Muriel Rukeyser, Thomas Merton and Gwendolyn Brooks, Robert Duncan and Marie Ponsot, Denise Levertov and William Bronk, Cid Corman and Carolyn Kizer, Jack Spicer and James Merrill, Stanley Moss and Edward Dorn, Adrienne Rich and Gary Snyder, Sylvia Plath and LeRoi Jones, Jean Valentine and Clayton Eshelman.

"Yet still the emotion that beckons me on is indubitably the pursuit of an ideal social self, of a self that is at least worthy of approving recognition by the highest possible judging companion, if such companion there be," Carruth quotes William James in an epigraph to *The Oldest Killed Lake in North America*. Carruth's work has been defined, in part, by two primary realities of American politics since World War II: the imperial power of the state and violence. In one of his earliest poems, "On a Certain Engagement South of Seoul," the poet presents his political morality: "The nations undertake / Another campaign now, in another land, / A stranger land perhaps. And we forsake / The miseries there that we can't understand / Just as we always have. Yet still my glimpse / Of a scene on the distant field can make my hand / Tremble again . . . I know when I walk out-of-doors / I have a sorrow not wholly mine, but another's." The poetry directly confronts the destruction caused by the military-industrial state:

> One night the water lay so deathly still
> that the factories' constellated lights on the other shore,
> the mills and refineries, made gleaming wires
> across the surface, a great fallen and silent
> harp; and the moon, huge and orange,
> shuddered behind the trembling many-petaled efflorescence
> on the stalks of the chimneys, white mortuary flowers.
> Really, from the nearer shore on the highway to Liverpool,
> one saw the kind of splendor that lasts forever.

Listen to a voice speaking of liberty from "Paragraphics," a poem in sequence in *Brothers, I Loved You All*:

> "I am a fanatic lover of liberty, considering it
> the unique condition in which intelligence, dignity,
> and human happiness may develop and grow;
> not the purely formal liberty

conceded, measured out, and regulated by the State;
an eternal lie which in reality represents
nothing more than the privilege
of some founded on the slavery
of the rest; not the individualistic, egoistic,
shabby and fictitious liberty
extolled by the school of J. J. Rousseau and the other
schools of bourgeois liberalism."

Or this, from Carruth's *Sonnets:*

"All revolutions in modern times have led
to a reinforcement of the power of the State."
Cindy, this is the stunner. Granted, what
we, being rebels, must do is easy (fed
to our ears): decline, disacquiescence. Our head
is straight. But our life? An aimless fate
has brought us to live in a system more absolute
than any kingdom, for now the State is god,
total annihilation being its sign and power,
and when all heads, past, present, and to come,
have been smithereened will it matter that some
were straight? Will it help in life's final hour?
No, it will not help. Then only love
will help, and the suffering it is made of.

Political order is grounded on the suffering that love is made of;
Carruth knows both private and public sorrows:

Very fast. First, tension
In legs and neck, the flutter
Of hand to head; then
The general tremor, upheaval
Sense of wobbling, falling;
Then panic, desperation.
To run, to fly, to sink—
To escape: an absolute command.
Fear of screaming, the sound
Bulging in the throat.
Heart-gasp and darkness
At the edge of the eyes.
Fear of fear. Terror is

Such a humiliating spectacle.
In busses, offices, theaters,
Shops, country roads and
Lonely woods, everywhere
But in bedrooms and barrooms.
William James spoke
Of the experience and ascribed
It to an acute perception
Of evil—or some such;
I have no books. Yes,
Perception is involved,
A sharp sensory receptivity
To almost hidden things,
And evil of course is also
Involved, for you learn quickly
In fear nature's rapacities.

From these few lines—taken out of context from *The Bloom-ingdale Papers*—it's clear how grounded a poet Carruth is: Fear is looked at objectively and subjectively, by subtle turns of perception and form, both socially and ontologically. The poet recognized early on—as in "The Buddhist Painter Prepares to Paint"—"But, alas, his sorrow / Is genuine, / The requisite of art." The making of the poem turns pain and suffering into an act of beauty and love. At times—as in "Post-Impressionist Susurration for the First of November, 1983," from *Tell Me Again*—we hear this beauty and love openly declared:

Does anything get more tangled and higgeldy-piggeldy than
  the days as they drop all jumbled and
One by one on the historical heap? Not likely. And so we
  are all, in spite of ourselves, jackstraw diarists.
This afternoon we went walking on the towpath of the Erie
  Canal, which was strangely
Straight and narrow for our devious New England feet. Yet
  it was beautiful, a long earthen avenue
Reaching far and straight ahead of us in to the shifting veils
  that hung everywhere in folds, oaks clinging to their dry
  leaves,
Bare maples in many shades of gray, the field of goldenrod
  gone to seed and burnt-out asters,

Sumac with dark cones, the brown grasses, and at the far
   edge, away from the canal,
A line of trees above which towered three white pines in
   singular shapes.

Other times beauty appears on the borderline of transcendence:

You rose from our embrace and the small light spread
like an aureole around you. The long parabola
of neck and shoulder, flank and thigh I saw
permute itself through unfolding an unlimited
minuteness in the movement of your tall tread,
the spine-root swaying, the Picasso-like éclat
of scissoring slender legs. I knew some law
of Being was at work.

Then there is the matter of form. Carruth has been appropriately praised for his technical mastery. He has written expansively, even experimentally, in both open and closed forms (a study of his formal range and achievement is well worth any poet's time). Carruth loves to form and to reform the American language (which, for him, includes the languages of jazz and blues). Listen to how he does it in *Tell Me Again*'s "Meditation in the Presence of 'Ostrich Walk'":

Of the two cardinals the female is both bolder and more
   "beautiful." She comes
To the railing, crest raised high, snapping her eyes this way
   and that,
Uttering the nasal ech-ech of fear and belligerence,
Then down to the lower travis, then finally to the flagstones,
   where she feeds.
Now comes the male, seeing the way safe, and begins to hull
   seeds and feed them
To her. The mind performs its wearisome gyrationing. The
   female accepts
These token mouthfuls, but eats on her own between them.
   She is very obviously
Able to take care of herself. Although most people say
   Otherwise, and say so vehemently,

The difference between Floyd Bean and Joe Sullivan is
   distinct, crucial,
And unique. I move my hand to rewind the tape and the
   cardinals
Are gone forever. *Ora pro nobis,* my good St. Chance, my
   darling.

Pray for us, good, holy fortune toward whom the poet feels intimately: There is the poet's other voice—playful, tender, light—in love with his muse. At the heart of Carruth's desire for knowledge and reality—beneath the revolutions of his and our world—is a love that connects him to those times and places, whether in darkness or in light, which he so intensely feels. "Language / not urged and crammed with love / is nothing, while that which is / everything (at least in art)," the poet says. Or, as he says in "The Impossible Indispensability of the Ars Poetica," with great characteristic clarity and force:

                         No, what I have been trying to say
   Is that neither of the quaint immemorial views of poetry is
      adequate for us.
   A poem is not an expression, nor is it an object. Yet it
      somewhat partakes of both. What a poem is
   Is never to be known, for which I have learned to be grateful.
      But the aspect in which I see my own
   Is as the act of love. The poem is a gift, a bestowal.

Marilyn Hacker

I still remember the stir that Marilyn Hacker's first book of poems, *Presentation Piece,* caused when it came out in 1974. The combination of forms, styles, and voices was one thing: Here, at the age of thirty-one, came a major formal talent. But then there were Hacker's imaginative preoccupations: From the very beginning, Hacker's poems revealed the recognition of the fact that our deepest realities are who and what we desire. Her poems, unlike many, actually had other people in them; their world was one in which the great and primary emotional truths coincided and clashed. Blended into this intensity of emotion was a compelling appreciation of power and politics, and a longing for a social order (the sentiment has never been fashionable) based on what is human. The mix was explosive. No one had ever seen anything quite like it before in American poetry.

Selected Poems 1965–1990 includes work from *Presentation Piece* and from *Separations* (1976), *Taking Notice* (1980), *Assumptions* (1985), and *Going Back to the River* (1990) (there are no poems from Hacker's 1986 verse novel, *Love, Death, and the Changing of the Seasons*). I would have liked to have had a collected poems; having, for example, only selections from Hacker's brilliant sonnet sequences leaves you wanting the entire composition, but, still, Norton should be thanked for giving us this generous selection.

Selected Poems affirms what a few critics have said from the start, that Hacker, through a redoubtable, serious, almost punkish individuality, writes like a late twentieth-century American François Villon. This idiosyncrasy presents itself through a combination of rapidly changing voices that transmit direct, physical experience. These voices—which are terribly expressive—are always compressed into remarkable formal pieces. By grafting the talk of the streets onto patterns of "respectable" forms, Hacker shows us—as Villon did—that street talk is its own linguistic form, constantly revising itself in the city's corners. Hacker also appreciates that street talk is the most physical of our languages; no matter what voice Hacker employs, there is always something sensual about it.

"It is almost always / a spring morning, in the air a longing / to confuse myself," Hacker tells us in "The Art of the Novel," a poem from *Presentation Piece,* in which the poet also says, "I am inventing a city / in these lines." As in Villon you see, right away, that this is a poet who likes shape. In "Forage Sestina," for example, she chooses "words" and "structure" as two of the words at the end of her sestet's lines: "This is for your body hidden in words / moving through a crumbling structure," the poem begins. Another "Sestina" follows, employing "secrets" and "language" as two of the repeated words, filling the "crumbling structure" of the prior poem with sentences like "You tangled / my hair in your fingers and language / split like a black fig. I suck the secrets / off your skin." Everywhere throughout these poems is a language charged by formal means with utmost feeling—the poem as a separate presentation of its own time and space, its own act of real, complicated, endlessly desired invention.

This means that even when Hacker is using traditional forms, the results are something else. There has been a lot of debate about form during the past decade, about whether a poet should use, or should know how to use, metrical, rhyming, stanzaic "forms" that have developed in English and its progeny languages. Part of Hacker's genius is her use of traditional forms, or variations on them, as an integral level of imaginative expression. Even some of her admirers have had difficulty seeing how her use of form relates to the emotionally pitched, polyphonic talk of her poems, which sometimes includes overtly value-ridden race, class, and gender talk (feminist, socialist, gay, in their ethical manifestations). Hacker has been praised, and condemned, for being too much the "formalist" or too much the "political" poet. The fact that she is both, and much more, eludes many readers, although Hacker has never been evasive about her ambitions.

The first poem from *Taking Notice,* for example, is entitled

"Feeling and Form." One of the persons to whom the poem is dedicated, Susanne K. Langer, produced some of the most important writing on modernist art as far back as the fifties, when, as a critical movement, "modernism" was first explored. Langer observed that poetry, like all art, is abstract in the sense that its form is distinct, an embodiment of the human feeling it expresses. Form has its own reality; or, to put it another way, form, too, is expression. For anyone who didn't get the idea from her first two books, in "Feeling and Form" Hacker says it straight—well, almost straight. The poem is written in the form of a canzone, five twelve-line stanzas with a five-line *envoi*, each stanza written with repeated end words. The end words Hacker chooses to repeat are "write," "words," "draw," and "like." (She also adds a final line after the *envoi* that uses all the end words.) The second stanza looks like this:

> . . . the woman who sent you her Tone Poem, who'd like
> her admiration praised. That isn't poetry,
> unless she did the work that makes it like
> this, any, work, in outrage, love, or lik
> ing an apple's October texture. Write
> about anything—I wish I could. It's like
> the still lives you love; you don't have to like
> apples to like Cezanne I do like words,
> which is why I make things out of words
> and listen to their hints, resounding like
> skipping stones radiating circles, draw
> ing context from text, the way I've watched you draw.

The collage effect of this one stanza is, of course, magnified by the tumbling collage effects of the other stanzas patterned by the same end words—you can't help but take notice of the transformed form, how it turns around the vocal shifts, the human feeling it contains. The collisions of languages—fast, slangy, switching, sharp, metrically complex—are as much the subject matter of the poem as the thoughts, observations, and feelings expressed by them.

Modernist? Postmodernist? Call it what you wish. Profoundly experimental in its use of repetition, word picturing, structure? Definitely. What happens in every Hacker poem is that form—

quite often traditional form—is part of what is being expressed and felt, as much a part of the feeling in a poem as the various voices of personal and social reality also present in it. This tension between "form" and "content" is endlessly complex, like those visions of separation and exile, love and reunion, portrayed throughout her work.

Norton has also published—with the *Selected Poems*—Hacker's new book, *Winter Numbers*. In it, the central motifs of her poetry—the inner and outer furies of the physical world and the ways in which poetry embodies them—revolve around, simultaneously, the destruction of one's own body and that of the body politic. Hacker's voices are more mellifluously startling and alive than ever. Positing that "sound more than sense determines words I choose, / invention mutes intention," the book's dialogical contentions take you right in. Hacker has been doing this so well, and for so long, that you hardly realize that what you're reading is major work. Especially powerful is the sonnet sequence "Cancer Winter"—"Syllables shaped around the darkening day's / contours." The textured compression of physical detail, the sensual world loved down to its essential form in language (and note the rhyme):

> All I can know is the expanding moment,
> present, infinitesimal, infinite,
> in which the late sun enters without comment
> eight different sets of windows opposite.

"Words crystallize despite our lives," the poet writes, which is only partly true. In this expanding social moment—in the infinitely challenging human world of the poem—Hacker's poetry like no one else's crystallizes our lives for us, too.

Aspects of Weldon Kees

Relative to his peers, Weldon Kees possessed an extraordinary visual as well as aural sensibility. He liked ideas and thinking critically. He had an attractive speaking voice and loved conversation. He also had a strong sense of the world around him and a need to know how it operated. He saw himself very much a part of his historical time.

Kees' compulsion for expression was unusually intense. During the sixteen or so years that he was active in literary and artistic circles, he wrote not only poetry, short stories, and novels, but also essays and reviews (on literature, painting, and music) for the most prestigious magazines of the time. For the University of California Press, he and the psychologist Jurgen Ruesch produced *Nonverbal Communication: Notes on the Visual Perception of Human Relations*, which Kees edited and for which he contributed droll captions that tempered its clinical tone (he also gave the book its cultural agenda and wrote a chapter on schizophrenic art). Kees made and exhibited paintings, worked on documentary and art films, took photographs (most of the photographs in *Nonverbal Communication* are his), wrote, staged and participated in plays and "revues," and composed and played jazz. At the end of his life, he had plans to collaborate on a screenplay with Hugh Kenner.

The relationship between the various genres Kees worked in would be a study in itself; so would an explanation of how Kees' techniques and strategies in one art form affected what he did in others. The transpositional use of techniques and strategies of other verbal and visual genres into the making of a poem is, in fact, what gives Kees' poetry its enduring distinction. Sometimes a Kees poem uses the knowledge, thinking, and language of a critical essay or review; other times a poem contains visual descriptions that have the impact of verbal photographs. Poems (and parts of poems) have the compositional "feel" of an abstract verbal design (at times effectuated, further, by the adept use of a "given form"—a sonnet, a villanelle, a sestina). Juxtapositions of imagery, planes of perception, and vocal play and sound patterns provide Kees' poems with a sense of compressed moving script. Every Kees poem includes a voice or voices nuanced by tone, shaped by strict or variable meter and (often) rhyme, intended to be heard on the page. These qualities define the matrix—the "field"—of Kees' poetic imagination; Kees blends and layers them stylistically into every poem, a style that seemed preternaturally mature.

"Statement with Rhymes," one of his earliest poems, is dated 1938. Kees was twenty-four.

> Plurality is all. I walk among the restaurants,
> the theatres, the grocery stores; I ride the cars
> and hear of Mrs. Bedford's teeth and Albuquerque,
> strikes unsettled, someone's simply marvelous date,
> news of the German Jews, the baseball scores,
> storetalk and whoretalk, talk of wars. I turn
> the pages of a thousand books to read
> the names of Buddha, Malthus, Walker Evans, Stendahl,
>   Andre Gide,
> Ouspenski; note the terns: obscurantism,
> factorize, fagaceous, endocarp; descend
> the nervous stairs to hear the broken ends
> of songs that float through city air.
> In Osnabrück and Ogden, on the Passamaquoddy Bay,
> in Ahmednagar, Waco (Neb.), in Sante Fé,
> propelled by zeros, zinc, and zephyrs, always I'm pursued
> by thoughts of what I am, authority, remembrance, food,
> the letter on the mezzanine, the unemployed, dogs' lonely
>   faces, pianos and decay.
>
> Plurality is all. I sympathize, but cannot grieve
> too long for those who wear their dialectics on their sleeves.
> The pattern's one I sometimes rather like; there's really
>   nothing wrong
> with it for some. But I should add: It doesn't wear for long,
> before I push the elevator bell and quickly leave.

What remains most impressive about the poem (after sixty years) is how its irregular rhyme scheme, variable lineation, spatial, temporal, and substantive juxtapositions, and densely layered meanings shape the poem's conversational tones into the poem's "form." Observation, emotion, and thought are—as you read the poem—made into a visible object on the page. This idea of a poem (present in Kees' poetry from the beginning) is similar to what Louis Zukofsky later referred to as the combination of "sight, sound, and intellection" into "objectified emotion." Look at and listen to, for example, the visual and vocal dimensions integrated into "For H.V (1901–1927)," another early poem, composed of two quatrains:

> I remember the clumsy surgery; the face
> Scarred out of recognition, ruined and not his own.
> Wax hands fattened among pink silk and pinker roses.
> The minister was in fine form that afternoon.
>
> I remember the ferns, the organ faintly out of tune.
> The gray light, the two extended prayers,
> Rain falling on stained glass; the pallbearers,
> Selected by the family, and none of them his friends.

Kees often uses the direct technique of a filmmaker, splitting a poem compositionally like a jump-cut, shifting planes of perception, while simultaneously changing language and meaning. One way he does this technically is by using a long dash. "Farrago," for example, begins with a strange, abstract language:

> The housings fall so low they graze the ground
> And hide our human legs. False legs hang down
> Outside. Dance in a horse's hide for a punctured god.
>
> We killed and roasted one. And now he haunts the air,
> Invisible, creates our world again, lights the bright star
> And hurls the thunderbolt. His body and his blood
>
> Hurry the harvest. Through the tall grain,
> Toward nightfall, these cold tears of his come down like rain,
> Spotting and darkening.

The poem is suddenly stopped by a dash—followed by a change of tone and of scene:

> —I sit in a bar
> On Tenth Street, writing down these lies
> In the worst winter of my life. A damp snow
> Falls against the pane.

—followed by a yet another language change which, almost imperceptibly, switches back into the earlier language, as the poem substantively works itself out:

> When everything dies,
> The days all end alike, the sound
> Of breaking goes on faintly all around,
> Outside and inside. Where I go,
>
> The housings fall so low they graze the ground
> And hide our human legs. False legs fall down
> Outside. Dance in a horse's hide. Dance in the snow.

Many of Kees' poems include characters, scenes, and some form (or forms) of dialogue, like prose fiction. Kees' four Robinson poems can be read, compositionally, as a compressed novella. (I've always thought of Robinson as a metamorphosis of both Daniel Defoe's Robinson Crusoe and the Robinson character in Louis-Ferdinand Céline's *Journey to the End of the Night*. Céline's Robinson—like Kees'—has no other name, acting as a "double" for the novel's narrator.) One can read Kees' poems with numbered parts similarly, as multiphonic, multidimensional, serial planes—or "blocks," or "scenes"—of language (a way of imaginatively structuring a poem employed by Robert Lowell in *Life Studies*. Had he read Kees, *Poems, 1947–1954*, in particular? I suspect that he had).

Much of the critical writing on Kees has revolved around his suicide and how his poetry relates to it. Words like "bitter" and "apocalyptic" still pop up to explain what Kees' poems are about. When used to describe a poet's personality, words like "bitter" or "apocalyptic" may be accurate (although, if dealing with a person as complex as Kees, their use, I think, lacks even elementary psychological insight). When used to describe the meaning of a body of work as complex as Kees', such words as descriptions of content are inane. Octavio Paz, in his essay "The Other Voice," says this about the making of a poem:

> But I do not believe that poetry is simply an ability. And even if it were, from where does it come? In sum, no matter what it may be, what is certain is that the great oddness of the poetic phenomenon suggests an ailment that still awaits a physician's diagnosis. Ancient medicine—and ancient philosophy, too, beginning with Plato—attribute the poetic faculty to a psychic disorder. A mania, in other words, a sacred fury, an enthusiasm, a transport. But mania is only one of the poles of the disorder; the other is *absentia,* inner emptiness, that "melancholy apathy," that the poet speaks of. Fullness and emptiness, flight and fall, enthusiasm and melancholy poetry.

"Fullness and emptiness, flight and fall, enthusiasm and melancholy": It is, I think, as good a description of the content field of Kees' poetry as any. It is also a description that may have no correspondence to what was going on inside Kees when he killed himself. Paz continues:

> The singularity of modern poetry does not come from the ideas or attitudes of a poet, it comes from his voice. That is, from the accent of his voice. It is an indefinable but unmistakable modulation that makes it *other.* The mark not of original sin but of original difference.

Kees made poems of indefinable and unmistakable voice. Look, you can still read him—literally, I mean: The language of his voice on the page remains vital and alive. Of how many of his peers may the same be said? Kees was forty when he died. His precocious talent, his great gift of reinventing, envisioning, and vocally forming into poetry the enthusiasm and emptiness, the flight and fall, the joy and melancholy of being alive—I always think of him as having been older. But the act of making a poem is, actually, after all, ancient.

Smokey Robinson's
High Tenor Voice

seemed to weave itself through the thick, hot June air, between the jazz-like piano accompaniment, the sound of an electronic flute, soft drums, the steady yet subtly fluctuating "funky Motown" rhythm guitar, and the full, powerful gospel voices of his two women background singers, who half-sat on stools before microphones. His voice seemed like an instrument itself, as did, strangely, the words he sang. When the band began the soft Latin jazz type introduction to "Baby, That's Backatcha," there were some in the crowd who stood up and began dancing (others sat, staring hard at the thin figure dressed in a gold one-piece outfit covered with rhinestones, listening closely as he crooned

> A touch of ooh and some ooo baby yeah
> What it is exactly you don't know but it is . . .)

When he sang, without accompaniment, the opening lines of "You Are the Sunshine of My Life," there were those who could not restrain shouts of yes—shouts that seemed to inspire the singer's voice to positions on the scale that sounded beautifully impossible. When he moved into the last chorus of "The Tracks of My Tears"—his whole body pulsating to the music around him, to the crowd (half of them singing with him), and to his own voice—one had the feeling that he was expressing a deep desperation, and that his body needed to move the music to a kind of emotional, cathartic conclusion. When he sang, as if it was a spiritual, the opening stanza and chorus of "Bad Girl," his first recorded song from seventeen years earlier, moving from it into the slow adolescent 1960 song "You Can Depend on Me," there were claps and appreciative remarks, almost personal, from those who knew the words and melodies by heart. One woman stood up and began applauding as loud as she could. The music, in its totality, had a way of taking hold of every sense; the intermingling of instrument and vocal in a coherent, harmonious rhythm went directly to that point in the human body where all the blood flows through.

And, it seemed, when he had finished his last song, "Happy"—the theme from *Lady Sings the Blues,* a song for which he applied lyrics to the melody of Michel Legrand—the crowd sat as if stunned, as if all the music of the previous hour had not yet been assimilated, as if the music they'd heard had become a part of the air around them. They wanted, it seemed, to take it all away with them, so that they could, when they wanted, remember again something they had remembered for the first time, as they listened to Smokey Robinson's high tenor voice weave itself like a musical instrument through the dark, thick June air that opened with stars, between jazz-like piano melodies, the sound of an electronic harp, the saxophone (its sound the sound of a soul's very self), the gentle, soft, almost rolling rhythm guitar of Marvin Tarplin, and the passionate, gospel voices of Carmen Twilly and Joyce Bradford, who half-sat on stools throughout the whole performance, giving their voices, through microphones, to the night . . .

—Journal entry, Detroit, June 1975

Joyce Carol Oates's *Blonde*

In *Moby-Dick,* in the chapter "The Fossil Whale," Ishmael proclaims: "To introduce a mighty book, you must choose a mighty theme." The theme of Joyce Carol Oates's *Blonde*—well, it's about as mighty as you can get. In an Author's Note, Oates characterizes the book as "a radically distilled 'life'"—the life of Norma Jean Baker, aka Marilyn Monroe—"in the form of fiction." But *Blonde* is no more a book about the life of Norma Jean Baker or Marilyn Monroe than *Moby-Dick* is—a novel? an epic? a fable? a high-seas adventure tale? a single sustained metaphor charged with meaning?—about a whale. A mighty book? I'll say. *Blonde* is one mighty, tremendous book.

A multitude of possible readings—where does one begin? Perhaps by asking how one writes fiction about a historical person who's been imagined at every level of our culture? Oates warns us not to look in *Blonde* for biographical facts. Yes, she has consulted a number of biographical works. But *Blonde* isn't intended as a historical document. Nor is Oates writing (as Graham McCann did in *Marilyn Monroe* or Norman Mailer in *Marilyn*) a subjective account of Marilyn Monroe as a mythic figure. *Blonde* is fiction, yet Oates isn't completely free to invent Norma Jean Baker / Marilyn Monroe any more than Don DeLillo was free to create Lee Harvey Oswald in *Libra*.

One thing: The mere ambition demands a book of epic proportions. After a "Prologue: 3 August 1962," *Blonde* plays out in five substantial sections, each corresponding to a period of time: Part I, "The Child 1932–1938"; Part II, "The Girl 1942–1947"; Part III, "The Woman 1949–1953"; Part IV, "'Marilyn' 1953–1958"; Part V, "The Afterlife 1959–1963." Yet, Oates reminds us, for all its length, the principle of appropriation employed here is synecdoche. Details are not used to provide facts but, instead, constitute the essence—the very being—of her subject.

How does Oates form the essence of this child, this girl, this woman Norman Jean Baker / Marilyn Monroe? Through the voice of NJ/MM herself. In *Blonde* Oates creates character and plot through one of the most complex vocal compositions in American fiction. NJ/MM's voice is, first of all, that of an omniscient narrator, speaking from outside of time. The omniscient voice is constantly changing tense and person, however, adopting the voice of other characters and observers, at times assuming an almost documentary quality similar to a movie voice-over. Yet NJ/MM's voice is also intensely internalized—an inner voice at once intimate, sensual, and ecstatic. Because the omniscient voice is also an inner voice, the reader never quite knows if what is being said can be objectively determined. But due to the force of the narration, we don't really care. What some critics have found problematic—how Oates's NJ/MM corresponds with our own knowledge and sense of her—really isn't. The voice Norma Jeane (Oates adds the "e") is so compelling we're immediately transported into the mystery, into the being, of *this* individual personality.

A voice above all—yet in Oates's portrait of Norma Jeane / Marilyn, the voice of an artist. One of the deepest metaphors in *Blonde* is the art of acting. As Henry James said: "To live in the world of creation—to get into it and stay in it—to frequent it and haunt it—to think intensely and fruitfully—to woo combinations and inspirations into being by a depth and continuity of attention and meditation—this is the only thing." This living in the world of creation is, in *Blonde,* who Norma Jeane Baker / Marilyn Monroe most profoundly is. The "Prologue: 3 August 1962" begins, "There came death . . ." August 5, 1962, we know, is the day that Marilyn Monroe died. The movement toward her death is what projects *Blonde*'s plot. But there are also two ontological visions simultaneously being plotted in *Blonde.* There is the *is-ness* of the omniscient inner-narrative voice, and expression of the essence of its speaker. Then there is the *is-ness* that Octavio Paz in his essay "The Other Voice" refers to as the "psychic disorder" of the creative self. One pole of this disorder, Paz says, is a "mania . . . a sacred fury, an enthusiasm, a transport"; the other, an "*absentia*," an "inner emptiness." Combined, we have "fullness and emptiness, flight and fall, enthusiasm and melancholy; poetry." Oates in *Blonde* suggests that this disorder—this passion—is in each one of us. Marilyn Monroe's "life"—as well as what we make of it—may just tell us something about who we are.

Character and plot composed through innumerable manifestations of voice—for example, Norma Jeane's "earliest memory, so exciting! Grauman's Egyptian Theatre on Hollywood Boulevard. This was years before she'd been able to comprehend even the rudiments of a movie story, yet she was enthralled by the movement, the ceaseless rippling fluid movement, on the great screen above her."

Norma Jeane on her sixth birthday, June 1, 1932, with Gladys—"Mother"—young and beautiful, who works at a menial job at The Studio. But there is no Father—who is Norma Jeane's father? Norma Jeane, who loved to be read to by Gladys because it meant more calm, not "sudden bursts of laughter, or cursing, or tears"; Gladys reading to her from *The Little Treasury of American Verse,* a poem of Emily Dickinson's: "Because I could not stop for Death, / He kindly stopped for me; / The Carriage held but just Ourselves / And Immortality." So, too, Norma Jeane her whole life secretly will name her own characters in the poems she writes, in her tragic—or is it comic?—play, her own invented movie script: Father, Mother, Fair Princess, Dark Prince, Baby, Magic Friend, Rumpelstiltskin, Rin Tin Tin, The Sharpshooter, the Ex-Athlete, the Playwright, Beggar Maid, the President. Mystery. Death.

In the City of Sand, Los Angeles—"built on sand and it *is* sand. It's a desert," Gladys tells her. During the fire season, autumn 1934, Gladys mentally disintegrates (she will be put into a state psychiatric hospital), a "crying sniveling child beside her," an eight-year-old with a stammer. There is no one to take care of her after her grandmother dies, so she is placed into the custody of the state. Norma Jeane—"I am so ashamed, nobody wants me, I want to die"—a girl of twelve, boys and men sexually aroused by her ("Look at the ass on that one, the little blonde!"), hearing, yet blushing and indignantly not hearing, taught Christian Science by the director of the orphanage ("That God is Mind, and Mind is all, and mere 'matter' does not exist"), self-consciously ashamed of her body, startled by her first menses, the heavy flow of her blood. Norma Jeane, fifteen, living in the foster home of Elsie and Warren Pirig, writing poems and prayers, her sexuality driving men crazy, involved—to what extent?—with several (some of them married), unsuccessfully trying out for the cheerleading team, the Van Nuys High School play (Thornton Wilder's *Our Town*), the girls' choir. Married at sixteen ("Where was the bride's mother?") to Bucky Glazer, five years older than she is, an embalmer's assistant who also works the night shift at Lockheed Aviation. Norma Jeane is "sexy like Rita Hayworth. But a girl you'd want to marry like Jeanette MacDonald." For Norma Jeane: "The fundamental truth of my life whether in fact it was truth of my life whether in fact it was burlesque of truth: when a man wants you, you're safe." Only a year later: "She's sucking me dry. She's driving me away . . . *And the weird thing is, I don't think she feels much, in her actual body. The way a woman is supposed to feel.*" Then the day that Bucky informs her that he's enlisted in the merchant marine: "No, Daddy! You can't leave me. I'll die if you leave me"—Norma Jeane clutching at him, moaning, her breasts pressed against his sweaty chest, trying to straddle him, smacking her thighs against him, coiled tense and quivering. "Stop it!" he shouted into her face, "Stop it! You sad, sick cow."

Eighteen now, living by herself, working in an aircraft factory—"She was a *working girl* now"—loading airplane fuselages with liquid plastic. Pain and fever and severe menstrual cramps. "Now there was no one who loved her. Now she was on her own, twenty years-old, divorced" (which she mentions to her mother—diagnosed "acute chronic paranoid schizophrenia with probably alcoholic and drug-induced neurological impairment"—on one of her frequent visits to the state hospital). Discovered by a photographer, "*as if whoever held that camera was her closest friend. Or maybe it was the camera that was her closest friend,*" and made into a Pinup. A Preene model and a contract player at The Studio. "The truth was, her life was hard work, anxious work." At an acting class she's laughed at: "*Your insides don't match your outside. You're a freak.*" A meeting arranged by her agent with the head of The Studio, Mr. Z. "*Who's that blonde looking like a tramp* one of my so-called friends reported to me Mr. Z had said of me." "Mr. Z pushing her toward a white fur rug saying, *Get down Blondie*"—and "the hurt of the Thing of hard rubber, I think greased & knobby at the end shoved first between the cracks of my buttocks & then up inside me like a beak plunging in." "Inside my clothes I was bleeding." Later that day, she's told she'll be cast in the movie. She will need a new name. "I am twenty-one years old & I am MARILYN MONROE." "Later that day the start of my NEW LIFE."

She is MARILYN MONROE when she falls madly in love with her Gemini twin Cass C (the son of Charlie Chaplin). She is Angela in *The Asphalt Jungle*. Who's the blonde? "Who's the blonde? The blonde is my client, 'Marilyn Monroe,'" says her agent. "M-marilyn is only a career. She hasn't any 'well-being,'" Norma Jeane answers him. Under the name Gladys Pirig, she is a student in a Renaissance-poetry class at UCLA in 1951, reading George Herbert's poem "The Altar" out loud to the class. "Most Promising Starlet 1951." In 'fifty-two, the role of Nell in *Don't Bother to Knock*. The release of photographs taken by the Marxist photographer Otto Ose in 1949: "The nude photos of Norma Jeane Baker, a/k/a 'Marilyn Monroe' he'd taken that day would become the most famous, or infamous, calendar nudes in history. For which the model would earn fifty dollars and millions of dollars would be earned by others. By men." "Miss Golden Dreams"—dropped from The Studio. Who tries killing herself. The role of Rose in *Niagara* is what saves her. She is famous. Lover now both to Cass C and Eddy G (the son of Edward G. Robinson)—Cass C and Eddy G are lovers, too. Pregnant by one of them (which one she doesn't know). At the party following the *Niagara* premiere, confronting Mr. Z., in Rose's mocking undertone: "Do you remember that day in September 1947? I was just a girl. I was so scared! I hadn't yet been given my Studio name. Do you remember hurting me, Mr. Z? . . . Years ago. And then you dropped my contract, Mr. Z. Do you remember?"

Mother's health is deteriorating. She worries about Baby. She is the talk of the media. Rumors she's had sex with hundreds of men. Rumors she's a Benzedrine junkie. She meets the Ex-Athlete, who asked to meet her. The day that she looks for a place to live for Baby and her with Cass C and Eddy G, Cass C nearly dead from a drug overdose—"she knew what she would do." The role of Loreli Lee in *Gentlemen Prefer Blondes* (*"For this you killed your baby"*). She begins to receive letters signed "Father." *"I can't fail I must die. This had been Marilyn's secret no one knew. After the Operation. After Baby was taken from her. Her punishment was throbbing uterine pain."* Prescribed codeine (for "real or imagined pain"), Benzedrine (for "quick energy"), Nembutal (for "deep dreamless" and "conscienceless" sleep). In January 'fifty-four, she and the Ex-Athlete marry (nine months later they're divorced). They visit Japan, the eerie chanting outside their hotel window for Marilyn: *Mon-chan! Mon-chan! Mon-chan!* "The American Goddess of Love on the Subway Grating, New York City 1954," a "lush-bodied girl in the prime of her physical beauty. In an ivory georgette crepe sundress with a halter top that gathers her breasts up in soft undulating folds of the fabric. She's standing with bare legs apart on a New York subway grating." "Whore! Are you proud? Showing your crotch like that, on the street! My wife!"—the Ex-Athlete, insane with rage, hits her.

Summer 1955 she tries to drown herself. She leaves Los Angeles to live in New York City. She meets the Playwright at the New York Ensemble of Theatre Artists. *"Of course, I love you,"* he says. *"I'd like to save you from yourself, is all."* He would *"rewrite the story of both our lives. Not tragic but American epic!"* A decade later, still grieving, he would write: *"The intersection between private pathology and the insatiable appetite of a capitalist-consumer culture. How can we understand this mystery? This obscenity?"* She is Cherie, 1956, in *Bus Stop.* "What was happening in Arizona on the Bus Stop location, what had happened in Los Angeles, what she could not tell her lover was a strangeness too elusive to be named." She is pregnant and she miscarries. She is Sugar Kane in *Some Like It Hot,* 1959, in 1961 Roslyn in *The Misfits.* A quotation from Pascal is written in her notebook: "Our nature consists in motion; complete rest is death . . . The charm of fame is so great that we revere every object to which it is attached, even death." She watches a Marilyn Monroe look-alike onstage at the Club Zuma. *"Darling,"* the Playwright still calls her—"Hadn't she killed this man's love for her by now?" The remaining scenes include: "Divorce (Retake)"; "My House. My Journey"; "The President's Pimp"; "The Prince and the Beggar Maid"; "The President and the Blond Actress: The

Rendezvous" (Whitey, her makeup man and most loyal friend: *"Miss Monroe what has happened to you since your trip . . . in April, oh what has happened?"*); "Happy Birthday, Mr. President"; "Special Delivery 3 August 1962." The book concludes—a fatal injection of liquid Nembutal by The Sharpshooter sinking "the six-inch needle to the hilt into her heart"?—with a chapter titled "We Are All Gone Into the World of Light."

Seven hundred and thirty-eight pages textured with cultural, psychical, and aesthetic meaning: A critical commentary cannot begin to touch the experience of reading a book of *Blonde's* magnitude. In *The Nation's* pages in 1990, Henry Louis Gates, Jr., in his review of Oates's novel *Because It Is Bitter, and Because It Is My Heart,* noted that in the late sixties (shortly after her novel *them*) Oates confessed to the ambition of putting the whole world in her fiction, an ambition she termed "laughably Balzacian." "It may have seemed so to her," Gates went on, "but no one is laughing now." Since 1990, Oates has written *Black Water, Foxfire: Confessions of a Girl Gang, What I Lived For, Zombie, We Were the Mulvaneys, Man Crazy, My Heart Laid Bare, Broke Heart Blues,* and *Blonde.* Oates has become most like William Faulkner: Every novel is a newly invented form of language, a deepening vision of America. No writer today has (paraphrasing what Saul Bellow once told Martin Amis) delved into the mysterious circumstances of being alive at this time in America—explored our entire social strata—to the extent that she has. Oates is perennially mentioned for the Nobel Prize. One hopes that the Swedish academy will not make the same mistake with her that it did with Joseph Conrad, James Joyce, Virginia Woolf, and Graham Greene.

Poets on Poets and Poetry

William Carlos Williams, in his "Author's Introduction" to *The Wedge*: "The poet isn't a fixed phenomenon, no more is his work." A poet's work "might be a note on current affairs, a diagnosis, a plan for procedure, a retrospect—all in its own peculiarly enduring form. There need be nothing limited about that." The work of a poet may be a response to "the most violent action or run parallel to it, a saga. It may be the picking out of an essential detail for memory, something to be set aside for further study, a sort of shorthand of emotional significances for later reference."

Frank O'Hara, in "[Statement for *The New American Poetry*]": "It may be that poetry makes life's nebulous events tangible to me and restores their detail; or conversely, that poetry brings forth the intangible quality of incidents which are all too concrete and circumstantial. Or each on specific occasions, or both all the time."

Durs Grunbein, in "The Poem and Its Secret": "Personally, I believe that what comes out in poems is the human devotion to the transcendental—with a simultaneous fidelity to this world's prodigious wealth of details. For me, what makes up the consistency of poetry's secret is twofold: a mix of love of this world with curiosity about metaphysics. The proof? Only among the poets does one come across those successful moments of reconciliation of something purely ideal with its unexpectedly concrete manifestations."

Octavio Paz, in "Luis Cernuda: The Edifying Word," translated by Michael Schmidt: "A poet is one who . . . writes because he cannot help it—and knows it. He is an accomplice of his fate—and its judge."

Marie Ponsot

A new book of poems by Marie Ponsot is an event: Its readers can expect that each poem in it will be its own brilliant world of language—a language that encompasses what makes us human—made accordingly to every possible measure of perfection. Ponsot has always written at the top of her talent, which is at the top of the art. From the outset, she has imagined the making of a poem in its fullest sense. A poem for Ponsot is an object of sight and of sound, of thoughts and of feelings, a created field of interacting language and themes, composed of various voices and tones of voice. Ponsot requires that we pay the closest attention to every level of language in a poem: syllables, words, lines, sentences, spacing on the page, punctuation, meter, rhyme, syntax. The payoffs—depths of meaning that endlessly surprise, instruct, and delight—are stunning.

Easy is Ponsot's sixth book of poems. Born in New York City in 1921, Ponsot graduated from St. Joseph's College for Women in Brooklyn and Columbia University, where she received a master of arts degree in seventeenth-century literature. After World War II, she lived for three years in Paris, where she married the French painter Claude Ponsot. Returning to New York, she worked as a translator from the French (including thirty-seven children's books and *The Fables of La Fontaine*), and freelance writer of radio and television scripts, while raising seven children on her own. She taught until she was seventy-two at Queens College, where she is now professor emerita of English. Ponsot's first book, *True Minds*, was published in 1957 by Lawrence Ferlinghetti in the City Lights Pocket Poets Series, which, a year earlier, had published Allen Ginsberg's *Howl and Other Poems*. Her second book, *Admit Impediment*, was published more than two decades later in 1981 by Knopf. Much was made in the poetry world at the time about the fact that Ponsot hadn't published a second book until she was almost sixty, but Ponsot had never stopped writing poems. During the late fifties and through the sixties and seventies, personal circumstances demanded that she take herself out of a post–World War II poetry business established by her peers, in which the norm for visibility and success was not only full-time self-promotion, but also the publication of a book of poems every two or three years. *Admit Impediment* was followed seven years later in 1988 by *The Green Book,* and, then, ten years after that, by *The Bird Catcher*—which received the National Book Critics Circle Award—in 1998. *Springing: New and Selected Poems* was published in 2002 to great acclaim, when Ponsot was eighty-one.

By the second poem in *Easy,* "If I Live, Stones Hear," Ponsot has brought us to her new book's vision: "Between silence and sound / we are balancing darkness, / making light of it . . ." she writes, releasing through her language (within three lines!) several meanings. "We," of course, includes every one of us, living as we do between being silent and speaking, between realities both good and bad. But, of course, "we" also includes the poet, who, now in her eighties, has spent well over fifty years "making light" of her and our darkness (whatever its source) by making poems. The theme is picked up forcefully again in "This Bridge, Like Poetry, is Vertigo." William Blake is quoted in an epigram: "In a time of death bring forth number, weight & measure." A cloud is described, driven by wind, "between earth and space. Cloud / shields earth from sun-scorch. Cloud / bursts to cure earth's thirst." The cloud, "airy, wet, photogenic," is "a bridge or go-between," as is poetry, which "does as it is done by." Or, as Ponsot writes in "Skeptic," changing her metaphor from a cloud to the sea:

> Language thinks us. Myth or mouth
> we migrants are its mystery.
> It's our tension floats these halcyons
> we want to say are safe
> riding the wave-swell,
> on the surface of the same sea.

Within the "tension that floats these halcyons," is, Ponsot tells us in "Language Acquisition," "a moving speaker, an 'I' the air whirls." In "Alongside the Pond," this moving speaker, at "the edge of vision," feels "just short of sight / pond air" that "shimmers pearly / unbroken ungated." "Bright / mist engages me," she says, "silent unmediated."

In several poems—"Head Turkey Muses: A Soliloquy," "One Grimm Brother to the Other," "Peter Rabbit's Middle Sister, " "The Wolf and the Lamb"—Ponsot makes light out of our lives in the form of fables. In others—for example, "Route 80, Salt Lake City to Reno, Beautiful," "Train to Avignon," "September in New York, Public & Elementary, 1927," "On Easter Sunday Bells Whacked the Air," "TV, Evening News—seen on CNN, autumn 2005, Afghanistan"—Ponsot takes us back in time to a specific place, where the poem transforms its deeper truths. *Easy*'s pulse is, as Ponsot says in "Against Fierce Secrets," "Heartfelt thought." "Drop your guard," she tells us, "keep clear, be slow; / double your careful opposites & grow." "True's risk"—she says in "Cometing"—"Take it I say. Do true for fun." Which truth? How about the poet's truth, the truth of language, as "words become us," and "we come alive lightly," "the jolt of language . . . its lucid hit / of bliss, the surprise." Or, as Ponsot writes in "Imagining Starry," how about the truth of "The place of language,"

> . . . the place between me
> and the world of presences I have lost
> —complex country, not flat. Its elements free—
> float, coherent for luck to come across;
> its lines curve in a mental orrery
> implicitly with stars in active orbit,
> not their slowness or swiftness lost to sense

In "Why Vow," Ponsot's world of presences in the complex country of ourselves and our language invokes Gerard Manley Hopkins, who "(some say, daft) holds / that his self is an unlost, a fact, / unchanged by its unfolding as it stands for his each act." Hopkins's "self (daft or not) lives out its vow: / his now is a perpetual now." Hopkins is obedient because "he said he would. /

He did as he said. He did / as he was told. He could / good as gold, hold good." In "Thank Gerard," Ponsot summons both Hopkins and Hopkins's God:

> God   to you
> hold him close-folded
> above his sillion
> Loft him Halo him
> Prize him high, pen in hand
> his two uprooted feet
> flailing awkward rain-streaked
>
> below his healing blooded knees.

Easy concludes with "Dancing Day I" and "Dancing Day II," both of which bring us to—as Ponsot says in "Migrant Among Us"—the "otherworld in this world heeded / so well it swims in close to us." "I call this the end of the beginning," she writes near the beginning of "Dancing Day I":

> In its mist, frayed ghosts of selves drowse;
> I call them my lost selves.
> Lately they drift close, unaging,
> watching me age. Now & then, one or some
>
> flare up, known shapes in known clothes.
> Each of them is not not me, and wears
> the clothes I walked in, joked, worked hurt in . . .

"I still know "—the poet says—"all those moves." "Those selves—they've "come to stay! / It's turning into a party." So, the poet puts out "bread, plates, glasses, grapes, / apples, napkins, pretzels, Bleue des Causses." Those selves come to stay "whistle old signals." Together in "our one name / we agree to our selving. I do agree." The poet proposes a toast—"why not." It's "Time to let go. / Get going. / Out of the cellar I take, ripe / the rest of the case of Clos de Vougeot."

"Once, one made many. / Now, many make one. / The rest is requiem," "Dancing Day II" begins. "We're running out of time, so / we're hurrying home to / practice to / gether for the general dance." So, "Here we come many to / dance as one."

Those lost selves "keep arriving, some / we weren't waiting for." "Every one we ever were shows up / with world-flung poor triumphs." Every one is "Glad tired gaudy," and "we are, more than we thought / & as ready as we'll ever be," all having "learned the moves, separately, / from the absolute dancer / the foregone deep breather / the original choreographer." So, now, the poet says, "Many is one" and "we're out of here." So, "*exeunt omnes*," but "oh," save "this last dance for me":

> . . . on the darkening ground
> looking up into
> the last hour of left light
> in the star-struck east,
> its vanishing flective, bent
> breathlessly.

The dancer, the dance, the poet, the poem: The famous last line of Yeats's "Among Schoolchildren"—"How can we know the dancer from the dance?"—comes, of course, to mind. Just as Yeats's dancer is the dance and the dance is the dancer, Marie Ponsot in *Easy* unfolds for us the ancient truth that the poet is her poems and her poems are the poet. Who in American poetry—except for, perhaps, Wallace Stevens in *The Rock*—has given us a book that so magnificently and so magnanimously portrays a lifetime committed to the art of poetry and all that it concerns? *Easy* easily confirms that Marie Ponsot is among our major poets.

Conversation with Charles Bernstein

Charles Bernstein: Welcome to *Close Listening*, ArtRadio WPS1's program of readings and conversations with poets. Presented in collaboration with PennSound, my guest today for the second of two shows is Lawrence Joseph. Lawrence Joseph is the author of five books of poetry, most recently *Into It* and *Codes, Precepts, Biases, and Taboos: Poems 1973–1993*—which collects his first three books, *Shouting at No One, Curriculum Vitae,* and *Before Our Eyes*—both published by Farrar, Straus and Giroux in 2005. Our first show consisted of his reading from these books. He's married to the painter Nancy Van Goethem, and he's lived in lower Manhattan since 1981. My name is Charles Bernstein. Larry, it's good to have you back on *Close Listening*.

Lawrence Joseph: Thank you, Charles. It's good to be here.

CB: Is identity something that's important to you as a poet? Do you think of yourself as a poet from lower Manhattan? as a poet of our generation? an American poet?

LJ: Yes, I'm interested—I've always been interested—in the way that poetry can raise issues questions of identity, and, more basic to that, issues of the self. Issues like the nature of the self; the nature of the speaking self; the types of language that deal with a sense of the self; and how a self, or selves, are expressed through various personal and social identities, have been aesthetic concerns of mine since the beginning of my work. And, yes, I very much think of myself as an American poet of our generation, and as a poet who, for over twenty-five years now, has written his poems in lower Manhattan.

CB: Gertrude Stein has that distinction between self and identity—identity is what goes on in the poem itself, while the self is the way she says, "my dog knows me," the way in which she would be described in a kind of socio-historical, cultural sense. Your work seems to reflect that, yet it also seems that, in the process of your poems, you avert aspects of your identity, while at the same time acknowledging them.

LJ: I think that's right. I do—as you say, in the process of the poems—avert issues of identity into issues of the self in the socio-historical, cultural sense in which Stein defines it. The self who is speaking in the poems is a self who exists with an identity or identities—or, more accurately, as a self who is identified in certain ways. The self or selves who speak in a poem are constructed through various vocal languages that reflect thoughts, observations, perceptions, feelings, often in terms of identity.

CB: Do you feel that there's some kind of core identity revealed in your poems?

LJ: The core identity revealed in the poems is the identity of the poet, within the poem, making the poem. For me—and here Stein's and Williams's influences are formidable—a poem is a composition, an aesthetically composed object, made of the vocal expressions of a speaking self, expressions of both interiorized and exteriorized realities. For me, an—if not the—formal issue in making a poem is how, compositionally, to express, to explain, both interiorized and exteriorized realities. It's how I read what Stein means to say in *Composition as Explanation,* how I read what Williams says in *Kora,* in *Spring and All,* in *A Novelette,* and in his prose pieces on Moore and Stein.

CB: There's another sort of non-dualism in your work that interests me, which is the relation of story to sound—how you imagine what you sound like, either in the performance of a reading, or how you imagine how you sound to someone listening to you read on the radio, or on PennSound's sound file— how you imagine the actual voice in relation to the ways by which you create the prosody of your work. There is an almost insistent storytelling in that voice, which, however, ultimately doesn't tell stories.

LJ: I prefer the word "narration" to "story," the actual voice, or voice, in a poem engaged in the act of narration, telling—to use

Stein's definition of narration—what has to be told. What has to be told includes the poem's content, which might be spoken in, among other vocal constructs, what I think you mean by a story-telling voice. How you tell what you have to tell is, of course, the poem's form, which, of course, includes its prosody. Narration tells—but what does it tell, and how? For me, a poem's telling is in the voice or voices of compressed, condensed, thoughts, feeling, observations, perceptions—compression that is achieved by employing various sorts of refracted language, including prosody—what Stein and Williams called "grammar."

CB: There's something about your work that's also very dramatic, but which doesn't have any of the conventions of drama. It's almost drama through the insistence of the sound, as a pulsing phenomenon through the exploration of the work, a dramatic sense that's not like a play, or anything like that—there's never any resolution in a traditional dramatic way. Your poems are lyric poems, actually—though the dramatic sense in them moves against—is in tension with—their lyric sense.

LJ: Stevens wrote in his commonplace book in 1938—he was fifty-nine—that a poet's poems are "speeches from the drama of the time in which he is living." Speeches from the drama of the time in which the poet is living—but, as poems, composed in compressed, emotionally charged language, made into an object, the poem. Yes, that's Pound and Bunting, and yes, it's Zukofsky's "objectified emotion endures," which Ginsburg had as one of the primary rules of his poetics. I want to be as precise as I can be here—let me paraphrase Stevens. A poem is a verbal object that tells the dramas of the time during which the poet is making the poem—a vocally constructed, verbal object, composed of the compressed, emotionally charged sounds of the dramas of the time in which he or she is living. I don't know if that answers you question (*laughing*).

CB: Well, it does, but beyond that . . .

LJ: It's difficult to describe. I love sound. I believe that poets have to—perhaps above all have to—love sound. I think that's where each of us imaginatively begins, where we start. I love the way that sound operates in language. But I love a lot of other things about language, too, the various kinds of pleasures that language gives. But the pleasures of sound are, I believe, integral to poetry. If a poem doesn't display a feeling of the pleasures of sound—the kinds of pleasures of sound that prose, finally, cannot provide—it doesn't fit into what I feel poetry is.

CB: One kind of sound that I feel from your work is—and maybe this is related to *Lawyerland,* and maybe folds back into my hearing of your poems—is a sense of almost being pulled over to the side and having somebody tell you something very urgent. Talk to me about how *Lawyerland* corresponds to that—not in terms of the book itself, the quality it has of sitting down with a bunch of crazed, manic lawyers and hearing them talk about law and lawyers, but in terms of the book's poetics, the poetics behind the people who talk in the book.

LJ: The book is a book of vocal compositions. A book that had a significant influence on the way that I composed it is Stein's *Brewsie and Willie,* one of her books with overt social and political content. It was her last major prose work, and she thought that it was her last great experiment, that she had finally succeeded in what she wanted to do with narration. While I was writing *Lawyerland,* I became intrigued by what Stein did with intricate forms of circular, storytelling voices—what she also does in *Wars I Have Seen,* another book overtly charged with social and political content, and, I might add, issues of identity and self. Another way of describing *Lawyerland* is as a *récit* —what Camus said that his *La Chute,* another favorite book of mine, is. *Lawyerland* is voices. I think that what you're picking up on—in what you describe as the urgency of the language—is . . . the word that I use to describe it is intensity. The word that used to be used is passion or enthusiasm—terms that come out of certain kinds of theater and drama.

CB: The reason that I wouldn't say enthusiasm is that . . .
LJ: Well, enthusiasm in the Greek sense . . .

CB: (*Laughing*) In the Greek sense, maybe. But in the New York City sense?
LJ: The New York City sense?

CB: Because it's dark . . .

LJ: Well, it is and it isn't. There are parts of the book that are dark in the sense that I think that you mean. But the urgency, the intensity, the enthusiasm of the book's language—the plays of Euripides, for example, with their choral poems and their multiple voices spoken by multiple characters create an intense sense of urgency, which is all that I mean by the Greek sense of enthusiasm. I like intensity in language. Intensity, and how intensity is expressed and formed, is an imaginative quality that I insistently explore. I like to—I need to—get the feeling of an actual voice or voices on to the page. If I manage to do that, the poems, then, if read out loud or performed, work that way, too. Getting the feeling of an actual voice on to the page is, after all, a performative act.

CB: Did you feel that *Lawyerland* sort of changed your work after you wrote it?

LJ: No, not really. I wrote *Lawyerland* after I'd written three books of poems—the imaginative sense of vocal composition in *Lawyerland* is in my poems from the first poem in my first book, which I wrote almost forty years ago. *Lawyerland* is a poet's prose book—the way that I had to tell what I had to tell was in prose. I wanted to create a language of law that had never been created before, the way that a poet of our generation would. You can read the book as one person speaking in multiple voices, while, at the same time, you can read it as a book of interviews that anyone could pick up and read as simply that. One of the book's ambitions was to make it operate at a deceptively profound aesthetic level—which, of course, is a poet's instinct—while, at the same time, having it operate on various, different, multiple, interpretive levels—which, of course, is also a poetic instinct. Poems operate at every level of language. If you write in prose and intend that what you write not to be read as a poem, you then have to make compositional choices very different than those you make when you're writing a poem.

CB: Can you talk about one or two poems, in some detail? The genesis of them? Some context for writing them?

LJ: Well, the reading that I did . . . whenever, these days, I do readings, I put together—depending on how much time that I have—what a performing vocal musician would probably call a "set."

CB: A constellation?

LJ: Not even a constellation. No, a set in the sense that . . . I've been listening to Bob Dylan—fanatically you might say—for over forty-five years. I have over a hundred bootleg CDs of live performances of Dylan and whatever band he had at the time, going back that long. What Dylan does when he performs is choose a set of songs from recordings of his prior work, and then he changes them, recomposes them. While I was putting together the set of poems that I read today, I was reading Wallace Stevens. There's a couplet that I found in a late poem, "An Old Man Asleep": "The self and the earth—your thoughts, your feelings, / Your beliefs and disbeliefs, your whole peculiar plot."

CB: From *The Rock*.

LJ: I really like his notion of his "whole peculiar plot," because that, to me, is what, imaginatively, the whole of my work is . . . my whole peculiar plot. So, for the reading, I chose poems which, read as a set, have a plot. I revocalized them, from the voices on the page to how I hear them now. That's how I hear what Dylan does when he performs. He, too, revocalizes each song, each a part of a set with its own peculiar plot. I read all of Dylan's work that way—the whole of his work is his whole peculiar plot. What is my whole peculiar plot? It's why I titled the collection of my first three books *Codes, Precepts, Biases, and Taboos*. The plot of the whole of my work—the story, what is being told in narration—is the codes, the precepts, the biases, and the taboos expressed in it. In fact, this sort of plotting is something I've always done, not only within an individual poem, but in each book in relation to each other book. I see myself writing—as Montale did, and as Zukofsky did—writing, plotting, one long poem. When I wrote *Lawyerland*, I was very much aware of how it would, as a book, fit into the books I'd written at the time, and, in writing the poems in *Into It*, I was very much aware of how, as a book, it related not only to my first three books of poems, but also to *Lawyerland*. The poems that I chose to read today are from my second, third, and fourth books. The poem that I began with, "In an Age of Post-capitalism," is from my second book, *Curriculum Vitae*. The poem's set in lower Manhattan in the mid-1980s, where Nancy and I lived from 1983 until 1994 on Water Street, before we moved to Battery Park City. We lived very close to the Brooklyn Bridge, "the Bridge" in the poem. I then read the title poem of *Curriculum Vitae*, in which I vocally plot various identities and selves—beginning with an Arab-American identity (my grand-parents were Lebanese and Syrian immigrants to Detroit al-most a hundred years ago, my parents were born at the end of World War I in Detroit and lived their entire lives there). That identity is picked up in "About This," a poem from my third book, *Before Our Eyes*, which is set in Manhattan during the first Gulf War. Then, in the poems that I read from *Into It*—implicit in them is a biographical plot, the fact that Nancy and I since 1994 have lived a block from what has become known as "Ground Zero." A consistent plot throughout the poems that I read is violence—the darkness, perhaps, that you were refer-ring to as a quality of *Lawyerland*, which, also . . .

CB: That darkness is not just inside you, but it's in the world that you're in . . .
LJ: Yes—the relationship between the world that I live in and its violence, and the terrible pressures of this violence on us, as in-dividuals and collectively. The feelings of darkness that come from this violence are set against other storylines, or narrations, or plots, including, crucially—and I emphasize crucially—those of beauty and of love.

CB: Do you think there's a way out of that darkness? Not for you as a poet, but for all of us, in some historical way?
LJ: I don't read history that way—I don't read human nature that way. I think there are times when the pressures of social violence are collectively eased, when, at least, we're not engaged in, for example, the kind of horrendous, corporatist, statist killing and murder that we've been engaged in. But I was, as you were, too . . . we're of a generation of American poets born into

a period of unparalleled violence on this planet. We were born three, four years after the dropping of two atomic bombs, after the mass killing of over a hundred million people. Our entire lifetimes up to this point—as we enter into our sixties—have been in a state of collectively accepted permanent war. As poets during this time, writing in the American language—well, it has to be dealt with, it has to be told, one way or another. The time during which we've lived—now, too, with its radical technological changes—is a part of our language, a part of our sensibilities, a part of our imaginations, a part of our poetics.

CB: Going back to readership, the strange thing is that the fact that you're a lawyer, too, and that you can speak a lawyer's language, you're able to bring into your work a range of engagement with readers who aren't at all interested in what your work is about or doing poetically.

LJ: Well, the language of the law exists throughout our sociohistorical and cultural worlds, and I do know that language, and do know how to use it in what I write. A reader is going to read what I write—poetry or prose—at whatever level he or she reads it. The aesthetic, or poetic, issues are there, and an integral part of whatever I write, but I can't expect, nor do I expect, a reader to see all, or most, or even some of them. I do, of course, like when they do. I definitely write to an imagined reader who understands, or tries to understand, what I'm trying to do as a poet. But she or he is not my only imagined reader.

CB: Do you think that the poetry you write has a specific kind of social role in American culture?

LJ: I don't know. Probably not. I certainly think it's important that poems be written, and that they be written at the most intricate level of poetic aesthesis—what Stevens, again in a late poem, called *poesis*—because I, first of all, believe in the activity of making the poem, of having the poem made, which is, finally, for me, a kind of meditative act. If any, that is the specific role that I see of the poet in American culture—the poet is he or she who forms the American language in it most multifaceted, emotionally charged way. We are the ones who tell what needs to be told about the language of the time that we live in.

CB: So, to add to the other paradoxes, or, perhaps, agonisms, in your work, there's another interesting one—the idea of meditative action. Though meditative is a holding place . . .

LJ: Yes.

CB: The poem holding its own with, as you say, this intensity, an intensity against the system.

LJ: A verbal object that actively holds, actively contains, an intensity equal to or greater than the intensity of often violent, externalized pressures. Yes. To create in a poem the deepest pressures of language—spoken, sung, human language. That's what, I believe, poets do.

Working Rules for *Lawyerland*

These "working rules" were assembled from notes before and during the writing of the first complete draft of *Lawyerland*. It was within the scope of these rules that *Lawyerland* was conceived and written.

1. "Don't be confused by surfaces; in the depths everything becomes law." (Rilke)

2. "You know how much I have always meditated about narration, how to tell what one has to tell. . . ." (Stein)

3. Stein's *Wars I Have Seen*: Stories within stories within stories within . . . (narration within narration within narration within. . . .). A means by which to broaden and deepen (and concentrate) time and space (including the temporal and spatial dimensions of language).

4. "There are, it seems to me, two ways to tell a story, one is the classical way, the way you expect, going from one incident to the next, twisting and turning on the surface, in all sorts of movements, sometimes quick, sometimes slower, beginning again, for better or for worse, the way that cars go down a (one or two way) street, and then there is the other way, descending into the intimacy of things, into the fiber, the nerve, the flesh, the feeling of things, going straight to the end, to its end, in intimacy, in maintained poetic tension, like the metro through an inner city, to the end, once the choice is made, making it essential to stay in the same conviction, in the same intimate tension, once and for all, in the intimacy of life, to seize the story in this fashion." (Céline)

5. "high decibel language"—"language that visually pops off the page"—"language alive on the page"—"you make things happen on the page"

6. No one not a lawyer speaks in the book: The entire field of language made up of the voices of lawyers (including the narrator) talking to lawyers about lawyers and the law.

7. seasonal shifts—the "elements": the weather

8. imagined conversations—from actual conversations: more "real" than "real"; make the between-lawyer language real, actual, at the level of the best literary ("interview") journalism (Wilson's *Europe Without Baedeker*) (Didion)

9. —the "I": "drops a detail here, a perception there"; "sets the scene"
   —the "I": a "character" too (intricately), in the last piece especially

10. "The vital thing, then, to consider in all composition, in prose or verse, is the ACTION of the voice,—sound-posturing, gesture. Get the stuff of life into the technique of your writing." (Frost)

11. Only lower Manhattan settings: "mapped-out"; the "geographical" as metaphor (Harvey's *Justice, Nature and the Geography of Difference*): By condensing geographical space you pressure other metaphorical space (including the spatial dimension of language).

12. imagined readers: present and future

13. what a lawyer, as a lawyer, senses—what a lawyer, as a lawyer, perceives—what a lawyer, as a lawyer, feels

14. Fredric Jameson's essay in *The South Atlantic Quarterly* about the doctor character in modernist writing (replace "doctor" with "lawyer"). The lawyer character (including the narrator)
   (1) is one who knows "how to motivate plausible narrative intersections among people from widely different

walks of life, from utterly unrelated zones in the urban
landscape, and from different classes";

(2) is one who "has not merely the right, but also the
professional obligation, to penetrate . . . sealed and disparate social spaces, to visit the rich as well as the unemployed, to listen to the voices of workers as well as those
of bureaucrats and politicians";

(3) is one whose story is an "extraordinary vehicle for
the mapping of social space";

(4) is a "vehicle for knowledge and an instrument of
perception and social exploration . . . an epistemological
device."

15. Stevens: "By the pressure of reality, I mean the pressure of
an external event or events on the consciousness to the exclu-
sion of any power of contemplation. The definition ought to be
exact and, as it is, may be merely pretentious."

Stevens: the poem as a drama of the time in which the poet
is living.

16. Camus's *The Fall*:

(1) The form is a *récit* (a dramatic monologue with a second character who listens and who speaks only within the
monologue's context).

(2) The epigraph is from Lermontov's *A Hero of Our
Time*: "Some were dreadfully insulted, and quite seriously, to have held up as a model such an immoral character as *A Hero of Our Time*; others shrewdly noticed that
the author had portrayed himself and his acquain-
tances. . . . *A Hero of Our Time*, gentlemen, is in fact
a portrait, but not of an individual; it is the aggregate
of the vices of our whole generation in their fullest
expression."

(3) Nothing in the book that isn't bound by the moral,
by some sort of morality; a world determined by moral
issues.

17. —language that is revealing
—language that is revealed

Rule 1: See Rainer Marie Rilke, *Letters to a Young Poet* 39 (Stephen Mitchell, trans., Vintage Books, 1984). The quotation is also the epigraph to *Lawyerland*.

Rule 2: After she completed her last book of prose, *Brewsie and Willie* (1946), Gertrude Stein wrote in a letter to her friend W. G. Rogers: "I think in a kind of way it is one of the best things I have ever done. You know how much I have always meditated about narration, how to tell what one has to tell, well this time I have written it, narration as the 20th century sees it." John Malcolm Brinnin, *The Third Rose: Gertrude Stein and Her World* 391 (1959).

Rule 3: Gertrude Stein, *Wars I Have Seen* (1945).

Rule 4: See Merlin Thomas, *Louis-Ferdinand Céline* 81 (1979) (quotation is a paraphrased translation from the French).

Rule 8: Edmund Wilson, *Europe Without Baedeker: Sketches Among the Ruins of Italy, Greece and England,* Together with *Notes from a European Diary: 1963–1964* (1966); "(Didion)" is a reference to author Joan Didion's nonfiction writing.

Rule 10: Robert Frost, *Collected Poems, Prose, & Plays* 688 (1995).

Rule 11: David Harvey, *Justice, Nature, and the Geography of Difference* (1996).

Rule 14: Fredric Jameson, "Céline and Innocence," 93 *The South Atlantic Quarterly* 311, 312–13 (1994).

Rule 15: For the quotation beginning "By the pressure of reality . . ." see Wallace Stevens, *The Necessary Angel: Essays on Reality and the Imagination* 20 (1951). For the reference to "the poem as a drama . . . ," see Wallace Stevens, *Sur Plusieurs Beaux Sujects: Wallace Stevens' Commonplace Book, A Facsimile and Transcription* 56, 57 (Milton J. Bates, ed. 1989).

Rule 16: Albert Camus, *La Chute*, in *Théâtre, Récits, Nouvelles* (1962). For the epigraph from Lermontov, see Albert Camus, *The Fall* (Justin O'Brien, trans., Vintage Books 1991) (1956).

The Game Changed

That morning at around eight o'clock I went out to teach at St. John's Law School in Queens, walking, as I always did, from our apartment in Gateway Plaza, in Battery Park City, at the corner of Liberty and South End Avenue, a block from the World Trade Center, through the Trade Center to the Cortland Street subway station. I was on the R train by 8:15. When I got to St. John's around 9:30, I was told that an airplane had flown into one of the World Trade Center Towers. At my office was a voice mail message from Nancy. She'd gone to vote in the mayoral primary in the Dow Jones Building across the street from Gateway Plaza when the plane hit. She'd gone back up to our apartment and phoned me. She had the TV on—the report was that an errant plane had gone into the North Tower. I called and said— remembering the terrorist attack on the Trade Center in 1993— that she should stay in the apartment until she had a better idea of what was happening.

I went to the Law School's atrium, where a TV was on, to try to find out more about what had happened. A second plane had hit, this time the South Tower. I went back to my office and another voice mail from Nancy. She, too, had seen on the news that another plane had hit. (Our apartment, which is on the thirty-third floor, faces south toward New York Harbor, and west toward the Hudson River and Jersey City. Nancy could not know what was happening at the World Trade Center except from the news.) I phoned and told her to stay put. This would have been after 10:00, perhaps 10:15. I went to the atrium for more news and watched as one of the Towers collapsed. I went to my office, called the apartment—the line was dead. Soon after that, I watched the other Tower collapse. Classes were cancelled, the university closed. I called Garris Gregory, my close friend and colleague David Gregory's wife. David was in Chicago for a conference. David and Garris, and their son Davy, live in Forest Hills. I told Garris that I'd spoken with Nancy, and that I knew she was in the apartment and not on the street. Garris picked me up at the Law School and we went back to the Gregory's home and watched the news.

I knew the World Trade Center and the streets around it well. We've lived in Battery Park City since 1994; before that, we lived for eleven years on the other side of downtown, on Water Street near the Brooklyn Bridge. My poems often take place in this part of Manhattan, and the conversations that take place in *Lawyerland*—a book of prose that I wrote in the mid-nineties— are purposely spoken entirely south of Canal Street. I watched and listened to the news attentively, trying, among other things, to get some sense of what was happening on the west side of West Street, and, of course, I kept telephoning the apartment. I also telephoned for voice mail messages at work, the line there unaffected. I had calls from my brother and sister, and other friends, but no call from Nancy. I wanted to get into Manhattan but couldn't—no one could, by subway or by car.

The next morning I awakened early after very little sleep and went to see if I could get into Manhattan by subway. The F train was running, but only to Fourteenth Street (it was, though, running from Brooklyn, through Manhattan, into Queens). There were barricades at Fourteenth Street—I got past them by showing from my driver's license that I lived farther downtown. I walked to Canal Street, where there were numerous police prohibiting anyone from going any farther south. I was told that all residents south of Canal had been evacuated. At Canal and Broadway, several people who lived south of Canal wanted to get past the barricades to their residences, but couldn't. Two lived in one of the five Gateway Plaza buildings (not ours). They said that they'd left their apartments right before the South Tower collapsed, and that when they were on the street they got caught in the chaos of the Tower's collapse. They said that many on the street had been injured, unable to run, falling down, pushed, even crushed in the panic. I asked if they knew if the building we lived in had been evacuated. They said they assumed that it had been. They gave me emergency telephone numbers, which someone had given them. I thought, if Nancy has been evacuated, and even if she was injured while being evacuated (she has a bad knee and is unable to run), she would have telephoned me at St. John's, or someone would have phoned for her. I wasn't sure where she was, or if she was all right, and didn't know what to do. I had a pocket of quarters and found a pay phone, and dialed one of the emergency numbers for "missing persons" until—I gathered from her voice—a young woman answered, who, then, with enormous composure, calmed me down. Why did I think my wife might be missing? Because I would have had heard from her. What did I think had happened to her? I didn't know, she could still be in the apartment—anything could have happened to her. Like what? A heart attack, anything, I said. Do this, the woman said. Find a policeman of some rank and tell him that you spoke to me, and that I told you to tell him that you think your wife is in your apartment, and that she may have suffered a heart attack.

I went back to Canal and Broadway and said this to a policeman—he answered there was nothing he could do, that he had orders not to let anyone, under any circumstances, south of Canal. I approached a policeman wearing white—I assumed of a higher rank. I told him what the young woman had told me to say. I said it emphatically—I think my wife may have had a heart attack and is in our apartment. He went to speak to several others—it was now around 11:30. He came back and told me that two New Jersey State police would accompany me downtown. At Chambers and Broadway, the New Jersey police said that they couldn't drive downtown any farther. They stopped a New York City policeman on a motor scooter, and told him that a New York City police lieutenant had told them to make sure that I would be taken to where I lived, to find my wife. I got on the back of the scooter, the policeman asked me where I lived. I told him to go west on Chambers all the way to West Street, then across West Street into Battery Park City, then down toward the Harbor. When we crossed West Street into Battery Park City, we saw no one else. We drove down to the area behind the World Financial Center until the dust and debris—almost a foot high—was too thick to continue on the scooter. We walked to the corner of Liberty and South End Avenue—a group of police were there. I told them where I lived, that I needed to get to our apartment to see if my wife was there. A young policeman volunteered to accompany me. Our doorman was still in the lobby of our building. I asked if he'd seen Nancy and he said no. He gave us a flashlight and the policeman and I went up the thirty-three floors to our apartment. Nancy opened the door; she'd spent the night in the apartment not knowing what had happened. We packed basic belongings in carrying bags and descended to the street, walking south on the deserted Battery Park City esplanade to Battery Park, then walking across downtown to the F train subway station at East Broadway in Chinatown—the only subway train that was stopping south of Canal—which we took to Forest Hills. We stayed with the Gregorys until the end of October when we were able to return to our apartment, where we still live.

I couldn't write about it at first, not in poetry. I knew I couldn't and I didn't want to. It took years before I could imaginatively assimilate the 1967 Detroit riot and the effect that it had on me. I am a compulsive note-taker, and—now that Nancy and I were together and safe—I began compiling notes from every source that I could. Of course, I would incorporate my experience into my poetry: A subject of my poetry from its beginnings has been violence. Two writings on 9/11 that have struck me as profound are "In the Ruins of the Future," an essay by Don DeLillo in the December 2001 *Harper's,* and "The Mutants," a story by Joyce Carol Oates. DeLillo and Oates are able to write about 9/11 profoundly because they've always written profoundly about violence. Poetry is language in its most concentrated form. Poetry, among the verbal arts, can best address—to paraphrase Saul Bellow—the mysterious circumstances of being, the feeling of what it's like to be alive on this planet at this time. Time, of course, passes, and places change, and the intensity of an experience is forgotten. The emotional pressure of an experience, as Wallace Stevens observed, eludes the historian. It does not elude the poet. "To live in New York is to feel the pulse of the country," Valery Larbaud said in his study of Walt Whitman early last century. New York City, in Manhattan, south of Canal Street, is the pulse of the city that is the pulse of the country—the heartbeat of American power, secrecy, and violence, both historically and metaphorically. Stevens, in his essay "The Noble Rider," written during World War II, wrote, "It is a violence within that protects us from a violence without. It is"—he continues—"the imagination pressing back against the pressure of reality." The poems that I have written have always attempted to press back against the pressures of reality. Before 9/11, that reality often included the realities of downtown Manhattan. That reality now includes not only my own personal experience of 9/11, but our collective experience as well.

In 2004, I wrote,

The Game Changed

The phantasmic imperium is set in a chronic
state of hypnotic fixity. I have absolutely
no idea what the fuck you're talking about
was his reply, and he wasn't laughing
either, one of the most repellent human beings
I've ever known, his presence a gross and slippery
lie, a piece of chemically pure evil. A lawyer—
although the type's not exclusive to lawyers.
A lot of different minds touch, and have touched,
the blood money in the dummy account
in an offshore bank, washed clean, free to be
transferred into a hedge fund or a foreign
brokerage account, at least half a trillion
ending up in the United States, with more to come.
I believe I told you I'm a lawyer. Which has had
little or no effect on a certain respect
I have for occurrences that suggest laws
of necessity. I too am thinking of it
as a journey—the journey of conversations
otherwise known as the *Divine Commedia*
is how Osip Mandelstam characterized Dante's poem.
Lebanon? I hear the Maronite Patriarch
dares the Syrians to kill him, no word
from my grandfather's side of the family
in the Shouf. "There are circles here"—
to quote the professor of international
relations and anthropology—"Vietnam, Lebanon,
and Iraq . . . Hanoi, Beirut, and Baghdad."
The beggar in Rome is the beggar in Istanbul,

the blind beggar is playing saxophone,
his legs covered with a zebra-striped blanket,
the woman beside him holding an aluminum cup,
beside them, out of a shopping bag, the eyes
of a small, sick dog. I'm no pseudoaesthete.
It's a physical thing. An enthusiasm,
a transport. The melancholy is ancient.
The intent is to make a large, serious
portrait of my time. The sun on the market
near Bowling Green, something red, something
purple, bunches of rose and lilacs. A local
issue for those of us in the neighborhood.
Not to know what it is you're breathing
in a week when Black Hawk helicopters resume
patrolling the harbor. Two young men
blow themselves up attaching explosives
on the back of a cat. An insurgency:
commandos are employed, capital is manipulated
to secure the oil of the Asian Republics.
I was walking in the Forties when I saw it—
a billboard with a background of brilliant
blue sky, with writing on it soft-edged,
irregularly spaced, airy-white letters
already drifting off into the air, as if they'd
been sky-written—"The World Really Does
Revolve Around You." The taxi driver rushes
to reach his family before the camp is closed—
"There is no way to leave, there is no way—
they will have to kill us, and, even if
they kill every one of us, we won't leave." Sweat
dripping from her brow, she picks up the shattered
charred bones. She works for the Commission
on Missing Persons. "First they kill them,"
she says, "then they burn them, then they cover them
with dead babies . . ." Neither impenetrable opacity
nor absolute transparency. I know what I'm after.
The entire poem is finished in my head. No,
I mean the entire poem. The color, the graphic
parts, the placement of solid bodies in space,
gradations of light and dark, the arrangement
of pictorial elements on a single plane
without loss of depth . . . This habit of wishing—

as if one's mother and father lay in one's heart,
and wished as if they had always wished—that voice,
one of the great voices, worth listening to
A continuity in which everything is transition.
To repeat it because it is worth repeating. Immanence—
an immanence and a happiness. Yes, exquisite—
an exquisite dream. The mind on fire
possessed by what is desired—the game changed.

Being in the Language of Poetry,
Being in the Language of Law

I

The 1985 Tanner Lecture on Human Values at the University of
Michigan was delivered on November 8 of that year by Clifford
Geertz. His lecture, "The Uses of Diversity," was published in the
Winter 1986 issue of the *Michigan Quarterly Review*. "Meaning,"
Geertz said, "comes to exist only within language games, communities of discourse, intersubjective systems of reference, ways
of world making." Meaning "is through and through historical,
hammered out in the flow of events. . . . 'The limits of my language are the limits of my world,'" he added, quoting from
Wittgenstein's *Tractatus Logico-Philosophicus*. "The reach of our
minds, the range of signs we can imagine somehow to interpret,
is what defines the intellectual, emotional and moral space
within which we live."

The issue of the *Michigan Quarterly Review* prior to that in
which Geertz's Tanner Lecture appeared—the Spring 1986
issue—is, in the words of its editor Laurence Goldstein, devoted
to "Michigan's premier city," Detroit. "Detroit: An American
City" includes a poem of mine, "Sand Nigger," and a selection
of journal entries, "'Our Lives Are Here': Notes from a Journal,
Detroit, 1975." In January 1975, I moved from Ann Arbor—
where I was living and a student at the University of Michigan
Law School—to Detroit to live with Nancy. The move was made
abruptly: We had planned to wait until June, but in late November of 1974, shortly before Thanksgiving, Nancy's apartment in Detroit (where she worked as an artist for the *Detroit Free
Press*) was broken into, so we decided to make our move then.

We moved into the Alden Park, a 1920s Tudor-style apartment building on Detroit's east side beside the Detroit River. Next to it is Solidarity House, the international headquarters of the United Automobile Workers. I had two semesters remaining in law school and would commute from Detroit to Ann Arbor for classes four times a week. After moving, I began actively to keep a journal—which I'd done before law school—writing long-hand, or typing entries out on an old manual typewriter.

"Our Lives Are Here"—which I put together in 1985—was only a selection. Other journal entries from that year included, for example, on February 16, 1975: "The effects of the de-pressed economy, a depression. The city is changing radically in ways that are difficult, if not impossible, to read. The very real fear that the social fabric has irreversibly deteriorated." A note dated November 13, 1975 (with just weeks remaining in law school): "When all this is over, to organize my notes, and, then, to write. Subjects that have been on my mind: summer, '67, the riots, the store looted and burned; working in the factory (Dodge Truck, Pontiac Truck & Coach, Walled Lake Tool & Die, Plymouth Lynch Road Assembly, Chrysler Clairpointe); dad, in early '70, held-up and shot in the store; a poem about someone imagined, driving to work at six in the morning on the eastbound Ford Freeway—when? before the riots? or, now, wor-ried about being laid-off? driving to where? a factory—Mack Stamping?"

The day before that journal entry, on November 12, 1975, William O. Douglas, because of illness, resigned from the United States Supreme Court. Douglas had been on the Court since April 1939—over thirty-six years, the longest serving jus-tice in the Court's history. I was reminded of this while reread-ing James O'Fallon's *Natural Justice*, a book of Douglas's selected writings interspersed with O'Fallon's commentary. One opinion presented in its entirety in *Natural Justice* is Douglas's dissent in *Sierra Club v. Morton*. The Sierra Club had brought suit for a declaratory judgment and an injunction to prevent the United States Forest Service from approving an extensive skiing devel-opment proposed by Walt Disney Enterprises in the Mineral King Valley in the southern part of the Sequoia National Forest ("an area of great natural beauty nestled in the Sierra Nevada

Mountains," according to Justice Stewart in the Supreme Court's four-justice majority opinion). The issue was whether Sierra Club had standing under Section 10 of the Administrative Procedure Act to seek judicial review of the government's decision. The majority opinion held that Sierra Club lacked standing to maintain the action because it suffered no individualized harm to itself or its members. Douglas dissented. "The critical question of 'standing' would be simplified and also put neatly in focus"—he wrote—"if we fashioned a federal rule that allowed environmental issues to be litigated before federal agencies or federal courts in the name of the inanimate object about to be despoiled, defaced, or invaded by roads and bulldozers and where injury is the subject of public outrage." Environmental issues "should be tendered by the inanimate object itself." Valleys, alpine meadows, rivers, lakes, estuaries, beaches, ridges, groves of trees, swampland, "or even air that feels the destructive pressures of modern technology and modern life" should be "partied in litigation," to assure that "all of the forms of life . . . will stand before the court—the pileated woodpecker as well as the coyote and bear, the lemmings as well as the trout in the streams . . . That as I see it"—Douglas concludes—"is the issue of 'standing' in the present case and controversy."

I first read *Sierra Club v. Morton* during the summer of 1974 in an administrative law course taught by Joseph Vining. Spending an entire two-hour class on the case, Vining took us through its various factual and technical dimensions, and especially, with favor, Justice Douglas's and Justice Blackmun's dissents. Vining specifically pointed out the language at the conclusion of Justice Blackmun's dissent, a reference to "a particularly and pertinent observation and warning of John Donne," which, Vining added, Blackmun quoted in a footnote: "'No man is an Iland, intire of itselfe; every man is a peece of the Continent, as part of the maine; if a Clod bee washed away by the Sea, Europe is the lesse, as well as if a Promontorie were, as well as if a manor of thy friends or of thine owne were; any man's death diminishes me, because I am involved in Mankinde; And therefore never send to know for whom the bell tolls; it tolls for thee. Devotions XVII.'"

When, on April 19, 1972, *Sierra Club v. Morton* was decided, I was in the final term of the second of two years of postgraduate study at Magdelene College, the University of Cambridge. On April 18, 1972—the day before *Sierra Club v. Morton* was decided—I wrote in my journal (which I'd been keeping since arriving in Cambridge): "Poems—three categories: (1) threnodies ('on justice' . . . Jeremiah); (2) psalms ('on beauty' . . . Augustine); (3) 'conversations'('on morality' . . . Camus)." I had, by then, decided to return to Ann Arbor to study law.

Another standing case with a Douglas dissent was decided two months after *Sierra Club*, on June 26, 1972. *Laird v. Tatum* involved covert surveillance by Army Intelligence of antiwar and civil rights groups. In early June 1972, I took my examinations in Cambridge for Part II of the English Tripos, and then spent most of the rest of that year in France, reading, in French, Albert Camus, Simone Weil, and René Char, and writing—often extensively—in my journal. I returned to Detroit in December. During the winter and spring of 1973, I worked in Detroit at Chrysler's Plymouth Lynch Road Assembly and Clairpointe factories. I moved to Ann Arbor in May and began law school (in Michigan Law School parlance, a "summer starter"). I don't recall reading *Laird v. Tatum* during law school; I came upon the case in late 1990 during the build-up to the first Gulf War, when I looked at a series of Douglas's opinions dealing with the president's war-making powers. I have, since then, taught *Laird* every year in a law and interpretation seminar course.

Detroit figures substantively in *Laird*. 10 U.S.C. Section 331 establishes the statutory conditions for the president to follow to call the armed forces into action "whenever there is an insurrection in any State against its government." Chief Justice Burger, in his opinion in *Laird* for a five-member majority, wrote that "pursuant to those provisions, President Johnson ordered federal troops to assist local authorities at the time of civil disorders in Detroit, Michigan, in the summer of 1967 and during the disturbance that followed the assassination of Dr. Martin Luther King, Jr. Prior to the Detroit disorders"—Burger continued— "the Army had a general contingency plan for providing assistance to local authorities, but the 1967 experience led the Army authorities to believe that more attention should be given to such preparatory planning." The Army's covert data-gathering system—which came to light in an article in the January 1970 issue of *The Washington Monthly*—"is said" (Burger continued in the passive voice) "to have been established in connection with the development of more detailed and specific contingency planning designed to permit the Army, when called upon to assist local authorities, to be able to respond effectively with a minimum of force." Respondents in *Laird* (specifically identified only in Douglas's dissenting opinion)—persons and groups of persons for whom, allegedly, the army maintained files on their ideology, programs, memberships, and practices—included "virtually every activist political group in the country, including groups such as the Southern Christian Leadership Conference, Clergy and Laymen United Against the War in Vietnam, the American Civil Liberties Union, Women's Strike for Peace, and the National Association for the Advancement of Colored People."

The majority in *Laird* held that the mere existence of the army's data-gathering system did not chill respondents' First Amendment rights because there was no showing on the record of any objective harm or threat of specific future harm; respondents, therefore, failed to establish a justiciable controversy and lacked standing. In his dissent, Douglas first denounced the majority's implicit conclusion that the president has the authority to establish surveillance over the civilian population:

> If Congress had passed a law authorizing the armed services to establish surveillance over the civilian population, a most serious constitutional problem would be presented. There is, however, no law authorizing surveillance over civilians, which, in this case the Pentagon concededly had undertaken. The question is whether such authority may be implied. One can search the Constitution in vain for any such authority.

As for "the claim that respondents have no standing to challenge the Army's surveillance of them and other members of the class they seek to represent," Douglas responds that it "is too transparent for serious argument. To withhold standing to sue . . . would in practical effect," he says, "immunize from judicial scrutiny all surveillance activities, regardless of their misuse and their deterrent effect."

After law school, in May 1976, I began a two-year clerkship

with G. Mennen Williams, who, at that point in his public career, was in his sixth year as an associate justice of the Michigan Supreme Court. Williams, a Democrat, had served as governor of Michigan for six two-year terms from 1948 until 1960. In 1961, President Kennedy named him Assistant Secretary of State for African Affairs. In 1968, he was named ambassador to the Philippines. Williams was elected to the Michigan Supreme Court in 1970 and reelected in 1978. In 1983, he was named chief justice. He left the court on January 1, 1987, and then taught at the University of Detroit School of Law. He died the following year. The September 15, 1952, issue of *Time* magazine featured Williams on its cover. The writer for *Time* noted that when Williams ran for governor of Michigan in 1948, his primary political alliance was with the CIO's Political Action Committee, "then anchored by some four-hundred thousand members of Walter Reuther's United Auto Workers in and around Detroit."

My clerkship with Williams began with an assignment to draft two labor and employment law majority opinions, *Breish v. Ring Screw Works* and *Bingham v. American Screw Products Company.* Williams would discuss with his clerks the direction that he wished a draft of an opinion to take, and then give great leeway in the drafting process. If he was pleased with a clerk's draft, he would sometimes adopt it as his own almost verbatim. *Breish* (decided on November 23, 1976) dealt with an employee who was discharged for stealing a small can of cleaner from his employer valued at less than a dollar. He filed a grievance under the collective bargaining agreement between his union and his employer, and his employer denied his grievance at every step of the grievance procedure. The collective bargaining agreement did not contain a provision for compulsory arbitration. The issue in the case was whether the employee could sue for breach of contract. In his opinion—after noting that the case "brings into play a broad spectrum of complex Federal labor relations law"—Williams held that Breish could sue. *Bingham* was an unemployment compensation case decided on December 21, 1976. It involved a claimant who was laid off from his job in Michigan. He then moved from Michigan to Pineville, Kentucky, but sought unemployment compensation benefits under the Michigan Employment Security Act. The issue was whether he was disqualified from receiving benefits under the Michigan act if he was available for work in Kentucky, but not in Michigan. Williams, in his majority opinion, observed at the outset that resolution of the issue involved an understanding of "the federal-state system . . . grounded in the Federal Social Security Act, the Wagner-Peyser Act, and the Federal Unemployment Tax Act, together with state laws enacted in conformity with the standards set forth by these Federal laws." The court held that, under the complex array of these laws, Bingham was entitled to receive benefits.

In law school, the professors who influenced me most—Theodore St. Antoine, Joseph Sax, Yale Kamisar, Joseph Vining—taught what Karl Llewellyn had the insight to see in 1931, during the early years of the Great Depression, that, "at best," rules "set the framework for decision, and the bounds within which it is to move. No less important," Llewellyn said, "if there is the slightest doubt about the classification of the facts—though they be undisputed—the rule cannot decide the case; it is decided by the classifying." Legal rules and concepts develop out of factual situations that "set the framework of approach to any legal problem-situation"; the legal rules or concepts that develop out of a factual situation "set the framework of thinking about, or even of perceiving, the problem." Llewellyn saw that any legal problem can be characterized as a "field" in the disciplinary sense of the word—as, first of all, a space comprising a number of interpretative possibilities available within "the law's" set limits. The way in which "the facts" are perceived and stated determines how "the issues" are framed.

While I was working on *Breish* and *Bingham,* I was writing several poems that would be in my first book, *Shouting at No One,* published seven years later, one of which, "Then," opens the first part of the book:

Then

Joseph Joseph breathed slower
As if that would stop
The pain splitting his heart.
He turned the ignition key
to start the motor and leave
Joseph's Food Market to those

who wanted what was left.
Take the canned peaches,
take the greens, the turnips,
drink the damn whiskey
spilled on the floor,
he might have said.
Though fire was eating half
Detroit, Joseph could only think
of how his father,
with his bad legs, used to hunch
over the cutting board
alone in light particled
with sawdust behind
the meat counter, and he began
to cry. Had you been there
you would have been thinking
of the old Market's wooden walls
turned to ash or how Joseph's whole arm
had been shaking as he stooped
to pick up an onion,
and you would have been afraid.
You wouldn't have known
that soon Joseph Joseph would stumble,
his body paralyzed an instant
from neck to groin.
You would simply have shaken your head
at the tenement named "Barbara" in flames
or the Guardsman with an M-16
looking in the window of Dave's Playboy Barbershop,
then closed your eyes
and murmured, This can't be.
You wouldn't have known
it would take nine years
before you realize the voice howling in you
was born then.

II

Two years after Nancy and I moved from Detroit to Manhattan,
in 1983, I wrote "Curriculum Vitae," the title poem of my second book. Its closing lines read:

Now years have passed since I came
to the city of great fame.
The same sun glows grey on two new
rivers. Tears I want do not come.
I remain many different people
whose families populate half Detroit;
I hate the racket of the machines,
the oven's heat, curse
bossmen behind their backs.
I hear the inmates' collective murmur
in the jail on Beaubien Street.
I hear myself say, "What explains
the Bank of Lebanon's liquidity?"
think, "I too will declare
a doctrine upon whom the loss
of language must fall regardless
whether Wallace Stevens
understood senior indebtedness
in Greenwich Village in 1906."
One woman hears me in my sleep
plead the confusions of my dream.
I frequent the Café Dante, earn
my memories, repay my moods.
I am as good as my heart.
I am as good as the unemployed
who wait in long lines for money.

For over a year—from the summer of 1982 through the fall of
1983—I worked, as a litigation associate at a law firm located a
block from the New York Stock Exchange, on a case that appears
in the Federal Reports in 1984 under the title *In re Flight Transportation Corporation Securities Litigation.* The facts of the case can
be found in the United States Circuit Court of Appeals, Eighth
Circuit opinion, written by Judge Morris Arnold. Flight Transportation, a Minnesota corporation, provided air-charter and
other general aviation services. William Rubin was Flight Transportation's president, chairman of the board, and chief executive officer. In June 1982, Flight Transportation made two public
offerings of securities, selling, on June 3, 715,000 shares of common stock and, on June 4, 25,000 securities "units" consisting of
a debenture and a number of stock warrants. Drexel Burnham

Lambert and Mosely, Hallgarten, Eastabrook & Weeden were the lead underwriters. On June 10 and June 14, Drexel and Mosely delivered certified checks totaling over $24,000,000 to Flight Transportation in full payment for the two offerings. Flight Transportation deposited these checks in its account at a New Jersey bank. A few days later, on June 18, the SEC halted trading in Flight Transportation securities and brought an action against it, its subsidiaries, and Rubin in the United States District Court for the District of Minnesota, alleging that the defendants had violated the federal securities laws, especially the anti-fraud provisions. The district court entered a temporary restraining order and appointed a receiver. The receiver transferred the remaining proceeds of the June 3 and 4 offerings—some $22,700,000—from Flight Transportation's account in the New Jersey bank to a segregated, interest-bearing "escrow fund" account in a Minneapolis bank. On June 23, Drexel (represented by Cahill, Gordon & Reindel) and Mosely (represented by Shearman & Sterling, the law firm that I worked for) filed a class action in the same district court on behalf of themselves and all other persons who had purchased Flight Transportation securities pursuant to the June 3 and June 4 offerings. In August 1982, Drexel and Mosely moved for a constructive trust on the escrow fund on behalf of members of the public to whom they had sold the June 1982 securities, and sought a preliminary injunction against the distribution, commingling, withdrawal, or other disposition of the fund. "During the following months"—Judge Arnold wrote—"the litigation became increasingly complex."

In the fall of 1982, I finished a law review article that I began in Detroit. (Between the time that I completed my clerkship with Justice Williams in 1978 until we moved to New York City in 1981, I was on the faculty of the University of Detroit School of Law.) "The Causation Issue in Workers' Compensation Mental Disability Cases: An Analysis, Solutions, and a Perspective" appears in the March 1983 *Vanderbilt Law Review.* The article opens: "The causal relation between employment and a disabling mental or emotional injury presents one of the most complex issues in accidental injury and workers' compensation law." In the article's introduction, I present its various purposes: to "explore comprehensively the technical and policy dimensions in workers' compensation mental disability cases"; to clarify "the distributive and jurisprudential considerations that courts and legislatures inevitably confront in their attempts to resolve the mental disability issue"; and, a third, more general purpose, "to provide a method of technical and policy analysis that applies not only to mental disabilities, but also to other disabling diseases of unknown etiology, including cardiovascular and back related disabilities . . . which contain essentially the same kind of technical, policy, administrative, and medical causation issues as mental disabilities." The article concludes with a "perspective"—a proposal for "a legislatively created compensation system designed and structured to deal specifically with most of the technical and policy considerations in mental disability cases and cases that concern disabling diseases of unknown etiology," and provides "the structure as well as the advantages and disadvantages of this proposed system."

During that time, I continued to write poems that would appear in *Curriculum Vitae*. "By the Way," for example, begins with the following two (of a total of seven) ten-line stanzas:

> What I saw as impossible
> together. Only months between
> the factories, furnaces
> with hissing bronze pipes,
> smoke streamed across flat skies,
> and a woman named Mimi di Nescemi, who exits
> in black silk trousers, delicate heels;
> a man who says his name is Ra
> wrapped in blankets in a cardboard box
> on Gold Street. I tried to explain.
>
> On February second, 1970,
> at eight minutes past four
> my father in his grocery store
> perceived how desperate the man was
> —he'd kill. The bullet missed
> the spinal cord, miraculously,
> the doctor said. Everything
> eventually would be all right.
> The event went uncelebrated among hundreds
> of felonies in that city that day.

I also wrote "Sand Nigger" at that time, during a period of heinous violence in Lebanon. The opening part of the poem reads:

In the house in Detroit
in a room of shadows
when Grandma reads her Arabic newspaper
it is difficult to follow her
word by word from right to left
and I do not understand
why she smiles about the Jews
who won't do business in Beirut
"because the Lebanese
are more Jew than Jew,"
or whether to believe her
that if I pray
to the holy card of Our Lady of Lebanon
I too will share the miracle.
Lebanon is everywhere
in the house: in the kitchen
of steaming pots, leg of lamb
in the oven, plates of kousa,
hushwee rolled in cabbage,
dishes of olives, tomatoes, onions,
roasted chicken, and sweets;
at the card table in the sunroom
where Grandpa teaches me
to wish the dice across the backgammon board
to the number I want . . . Lebanon
of Grandpa giving me my first coin
secretly, secretly
holding my face in his hands and promising me
the whole world.
My father's vocal cords bleed;
he shouts too much
at his brother, his partner,
in the grocery store that fails . . .
My uncle tells me to recognize
my duty, to use my mind,
to bargain, to succeed.
He turns the diamond ring
on his finger, asks if

I know what asbestosis is,
"the lungs become like this,"
he says, holding up a fist . . .

and the poem concludes with these lines:

Outside the house my practice
is not to respond to remarks
about my nose or the color of my skin.
"Sand nigger," I'm called,
and the name fits: I am
the light-skinned nigger
with black eyes and the look
difficult to figure—a look
of indifference, a look to kill—
a Levantine nigger
in the city on the strait
between the great lakes Erie and St. Clair
which has a reputation
for violence, and enthusiastically
bad-tempered sand nigger
who waves his hands, nice enough
to pass, Lebanese enough
to be against his brother,
with his brother against his cousin,
with cousin and brother
against the stranger.

In October 2005, shortly after my fourth book of poems, *Into It,* was published, I was interviewed by Charles Graber for the November 4–10, 2005, issue of *Downtown Express.* Graber (after mentioning in an editorial note that Nancy and I lived a block from Ground Zero) wrote in his introduction that, in his interview of me, he asked questions about my "Arab-American origins," my "years of law practice and professorship," my "influences, the weight of history, and the poetry of post-9/11 Manhattan." One question that Graber asked me was: "Has your heritage informed your topic at all? Obviously it defines you to some degree. So on the one hand, one imagines you might have a greater feeling of connection to the specifics of the crime of terror, if only as someone whose identity is bound together with the very places from which this conflict flows. On the other hand"—Graber continued—"since you were Midwestern-born, raised Catholic, educated abroad, and are a long-time son of New York, are those 'Arab-American' labels more misleading than helpful in defining your perspective and experience?" I answered: "My Lebanese and Syrian Catholic heritage comes from my grandparents, who were immigrants. My parents were born here and lived their whole lives in Detroit. My grandparents read and wrote and spoke Arabic, and considered themselves Arab-Americans. 'Arab' too has become a metaphor, a code, and my poems track that side of America as well. By doing so, I also track other groups of Americans identified pejoratively by race, ethnicity, religion, or historical realities."

Seven years after I wrote "Sand Nigger," in a journal entry dated January 26, 1990, I wrote: "Paul Valéry, 'Poetry and Abstract Thought,' in *The Art of Poetry*, in the Bollingen series, from a lecture that Valéry gave in 1939 at Oxford: 'There is something else, then, a modification, or a transformation, sudden or not, spontaneous or not, laborious or not, which must necessarily intervene between the thought that produces ideas—that activity and multiplicity of inner questions and solutions—and, on the other hand, that discourse, so different from ordinary speech, which is poetry, which is so curiously ordered, which answers no need *unless it be the need it must itself create*, which never speaks but of absent things or of things profoundly and secretly felt: strange discourse, as though made by someone *other* than the speaker and addressed to someone *other* than the listener. In short, it is *a language within a language*.'" I also noted this: "'A poet has to borrow language—the voice of the public, that collection of traditional and irrational terms and rules, oddly created and transformed, oddly codified, and very variedly understood and pronounced . . . So the poet is at grips with this verbal matter, obliged to speculate on sound and sense at once, and to satisfy not only harmony and musical timing but all the various intellectual and aesthetic conditions.'"

In early 1991, I was asked to write a comment on the first Gulf War for the *Hungry Mind Review*. I began "War Afterthoughts": "Make no mistake about it: The Iraqi military state is barbarous, an affront to the dignity and inviolability of Arab life. But," I went on, "almost immediately after the Gulf War began on August 2, 1990, the president of the United States utilized his enormous war powers to amass over a half-million American troops, as well as hundreds of billions of dollars of armaments, within eight weeks. War, on America's part, was inevitably made. Socially the president showed how efficiently the United States could collectivize militarily (although in other social realms—wealth distribution, medical care, sustenance for the aged, poor, and infirm, labor—the abject failure of the state to collectivize its powers remains manifest)." Historically, I wrote, the president "reaffirmed that these United States have been, effectively, in a state of war since the late 1930s. After over a half-century, the war state so profoundly permeates the American economy and consciousness that ours has become a society in which ninety percent of its populace appears to have no moral problems with elaborately abstract (and media controlled) justifications for state-sanctioned violence. As for the moral implications of the violence committed by our Armed Forces in excess of that needed to dislodge the Iraqi army from Kuwait, and the disbalance between the amount of violence our Armed Forces unleashed and the values (political and moral) we purported to uphold—well, take a look, for example, at a recent cover of *Newsweek*. Without any irony, the lead domestic story 'VIOLENCE: Is It Mainstream?' is scripted beneath another headline, 'Apocalypse in Iraq.' Neither article imagines there might be possible connections with the other. The question of how much power our constitutional democracy should provide its executive and armed forces is not only one of the most crucial domestic political issues—it is among our most necessary moral issues, too."

During the summer of 1991, I wrote several poems that appear in my third book of poems, *Before Our Eyes*. "Under a Spell" opens with these lines:

Now the governor of the Federal Reserve Bank
doesn't know how much more he can take
while my thoughts wander outside me and can't be grasped—
I'm under a spell. While the prisoners
on Death Row whose brain cells will reach
the point of boiling water during electrocution

receive blessing through cable television
and presidents and commissars devise
international housecleanings
history won't recognize for years,
the precedence of language preoccupies me too
under the influence of a spell.

"About This," also written in 1991, begins:

I surfaced from my reflections to see
wartime. YOUR BANK ACCOUNT AND FUCKING COUNT

a sign on the mirror of Le Club Beirut,
an obvious object of interpretation during,

quote, the month that shook the world . . .

and concludes:

Enough of a shooting war, military
expenditures, there may be no recession.

Is it true, the rumor that the new
instruments of equity are children, commodified?

That the Attorney General has bit off his tongue?
Those are—nails! That maniac wearing

wingtip shoes, turning a tattooed
cheek, throws at us while we talk about evil

outside, over burgundy, at the Cloisters.
This is August and September. This is wartime

bound to be, the social and money value
of human beings in this Republic clear

as can be in air gone pink and translucent
with high-flying clouds and white heat.

III

In February 2009, on the panel "Six Ways of Looking at Wallace
Stevens" at the Associated Writing Programs conference in
Chicago (other panelists included Cate Marvin, Terrance Hayes,
Robyn Schiff, Maurice Manning, and Jay Hopler), I presented a

talk on Wallace Stevens. I began by noting that Stevens was a lawyer, Hartford's in-house counsel for handling surety bond claims, and, in fact, one of the most prominent surety bond lawyers in the country. I also spoke of *The Irrational Element in Poetry*, a talk that Stevens presented at Harvard in 1936, in which he asks rhetorically, "Why does one write poetry?" and answers that it is because "one is impelled to do so by personal sensibility. A poet writes poetry because he is a poet . . . and he is not a poet because he is a poet but because of his personal sensibility. What gives a man his personal sensibility I don't know," Stevens says and then adds, "and it does not matter because no one knows. Poets continue to be born not made." I quoted from a July 29, 1942, letter from Stevens to Harvey Breit, written just months after the bombing by the Japanese of Pearl Harbor: "One is not a lawyer one minute and a poet the next," Stevens writes. "You said in your first letter something about a point at which I turned from being a lawyer to writing poetry. There never was any such point. I have always been intensely interested in poetry. . . . No one could be more earnest about anything than I am about poetry, but this is not due to any event or exercise of will . . . it is a natural development of an interest that always existed. Moreover, I don't have a separate mind for legal work and another for writing poetry. I do each with my whole mind, just as you do everything that you do with your whole mind." I then quoted from a letter written by Stevens to Breit a week later: "Lawyers very often make use of their particular faculties to satisfy their particular desires." I read from an untitled prose piece that Stevens included at the end of his book of poems *Parts of a World*, which was published in September 1942: "The poetry of a work of the imagination constantly illustrates the fundamental and endless struggle with fact."

Two months later, Chicago labor union lawyer Thomas Geoghegan, in "Infinite Debt: How Unlimited Interest Rates Destroyed the Economy," in the April 7, 2009, issue of *Harper's*, wrote: "Some people still think our financial collapse was the result of a technical glitch—a failure, say, to regulate derivatives or hedge fund. . . . In fact no amount of New Deal regulation or SEC-watching could have stopped what happened." The problem, Geoghegan says, wasn't the deregulation of the New Deal, but that "we removed the possibility of creating real, binding contracts by allowing employers to bust the unions that had been entering into these agreements for millions of people and allowed those same employers to cancel *existing* contracts, virtually at will, by transferring liability from one corporate shell to another, or letting a subsidiary go into Chapter 11 and then moving to 'cancel' the contract rights, including lifetime health benefits and pensions." We then—Geoghegan continues—"dismantled the most ancient of human laws, the law against usury, which had existed in some form in every civilization from the time of the Babylonian Empire to the end of Jimmy Carter's term. . . . That's when we found out what happens when an advanced industrial economy tries to function with no cap at all on interest rates. The financial sector bloats up. With no law capping interest, the evil is not only that banks prey on the poor (they have always done so) but that capital gushes out of manufacturing and into banking. . . . What is history, really"—Geoghegan asks—"but a turf war between manufacturing, labor, and the banks?"

Several months before that, on September 24, 2008, I wrote in my journal: "Locating, historically, the time of the financial collapse—Friday, September 12, Saturday, Sunday, Monday—September 13, 14, 15. The *Times*, in Monday the 15th's paper: 'On Sunday, as the heads of major Wall Street banks huddled for a third day of emergency meetings at the Federal Reserve Bank of New York.' No one connects the fact that these meetings took place two blocks from the site of the World Trade Center, seven years and . . . one . . . two . . . three . . . four days after the suicide bombings of the World Trade Center Towers . . . four, five blocks from our apartment, right over here, in our neighborhood again."

Five years earlier, in 2003, I wrote "I Note in a Notebook," which is included in *Into It*:

I Note in a Notebook

Pink sunlight, blue sky, snowed-upon January morning.
The romantic restated—a woman and a man
by themselves, each alone in the other. Those
transcriptions of the inexpressible—perhaps

the experience of having heaven
is just simply perfect luck . . . That winter,
on Belle Isle, the ice floes, the Seven Sister
smokestacks. In Angel Park, a figure in motion,
muted reds and grays, clouds of light, and shadows
in motion, a freezing wind out of Canada
over the lake. A figure, in the factory
behind the Jefferson Avenue Assembly, marking
and filing the parts of the new model prototype
Chryslers, standing at a window, smoking a Kool.
Those with the masks of hyenas are the bosses,
and those wearing mass-produced shirts and pants,
among them my father . . . Cavafy's poem, the one
about how if he's wasted his life in this corner
of the world he's wasted it everywhere. What
is happening, what is done. Convicted
of rape and murder, he leaves a piece of pie
in his cell, believing he'll be able to eat it
after he's electrocuted—the fact that a compound,
1,3-diphenyl propane, forged from the fires'
heat and pressure, combined with the Towers'
collapse, has never been seen before.
The technology to abolish truth is now available—
not everyone can afford it, but it is available—
when the cost comes down, as it will, then what?
Pasolini's desire to make, to write, an intricate,
yet rational mosaic, byzantine and worth, at least,
a second or a third reading . . . An epical
turn, so great a turn—her voice in him,
his voice in her—the vista, a city,
the city, taking a shape and burning . . .

Also in *Into It* is "Why Not Say What Happens," a poem in twelve-parts. Part IV reads:

Screaming—those who could
sprinting—south toward
Battery Park, the dark cloud
funneling slowly—
there are two things you should know
about this cloud—
one, it isn't only ash and soot

but metal, glass, concrete, and flesh,
and, two, soon
any one of these pieces
of metal, glass or concrete
might go through you.
As she turns to run, a woman's bag
comes off her shoulder,
bright silver compact discs sent
spinning along the ground, a man,
older, to the right,
is tripping, falls against the pavement,
glasses flying
off his face.

And, part X:

Capital? Careful! Capital capitalizes,
assimilates, makes
its own substance, revitalizing
its being, a vast metabolism absorbing even
the most ancient exchanges, running away,
as the cyberneticians put it,
performing, as it does, its own
anthropomorphosis, its triumph
the triumph of mediation—
and, let's not forget,
it organizes, capital organizes, capital is
an "organizing,"
organizing
social forms.

On Friday, February 5, 2010, in the *New York Times*, in a front-page article, "Efforts to Settle Sept. 11 Lawsuits," Mireya Nivarro writes:

With a firm trial date looming for thousands of lawsuits brought by workers at ground zero against the city, lawyers for both sides are engaged in intensive talks aimed at settling some or all the cases. The first twelve cases are scheduled for trial on May 16 in Manhattan. But Judge Alvin K. Hellerstein, of the United States District Court for the Southern District of New York, who is overseeing the litigation, said at a recent hearing that a detailed settlement plan about seventy pages long had been drafted. "There have been intensive discussions going on looking to settlements of individual cases and globally of all cases," he said. "The parties have been working very hard . . . The settlement is complicated."

The lawsuits against ninety government agencies and private companies were filed beginning in 2004 by more than nine thousand rescue and clean-up workers who sued over illnesses and injuries they say stemmed from working at the World Trade Center site in the aftermath of the Sept. 11 terror attack . . .

. . . its meanings, as Clifford Geertz said in "The Uses of Diversity" in 1985, "through and through historical, hammered out in the flow of events."

IV

In my journal, on January 4, 1990, I wrote: "Ideas for titles of poems: 'The Constant and Endless Struggle with Fact' . . . 'Admissions Against Interest.'" On August 22, 1990, I noted: "'Admissions Against Interest'—ready to write it."

An admission against interest is an admission to the truth of a fact by a person, although the admission is against his or her personal or economic interests. It is an exception to the hearsay rule and is allowed into evidence on the theory that the lack of incentive to make a damaging statement is an indication of the statement's reliability. My poem "Admissions Against Interest" is in *Before Our Eyes*. It is in four parts. Part II in its entirety reads:

> Now, what type of animal asks after facts?
> —so I'm a lawyer. Maybe charming,
>
> direct yet as circumspect as any other lawyer
> going on about concrete forces of civil
>
> society substantially beyond anyone's grasp
> and about money. Things like "you too
>
> may be silenced the way powerful
> corporations silence, contractually"

attract my attention. The issues's
bifurcated. "Why divide the dead?"

the Foreign Minister asks, "what's one life
when you've lost twenty million?"

And if what has happened during my life
had been otherwise could I say

I would have seen it much differently?
Authority? Out of deeper strata

illuminations. A lot of substance
chooses you. And it's no one's business

judging the secrets each of us needs:
I don't know what I'd do without my Double.

V

So it is—"the reach of our minds, the range of signs we can imagine somehow to interpret . . . what defines the intellectual, emotional and moral space within which we live"—like this it is, being
in the language of poetry, being in the language of law . . .

UNDER DISCUSSION
Annie Finch and Marilyn Hacker, General Editors
Donald Hall, Founding Editor

Volumes in the Under Discussion series collect reviews and essays about
individual poets. The series is concerned with contemporary American and
English poets about whom the consensus has not yet been formed and the
final vote has not been taken. Titles in the series include:

On Frank Bidart: Fastening the Voice to the Page
  edited by Liam Rector and Tree Swenson
On Louise Glück: Change What You See
  edited by Joanne Feit Diehl
On James Tate
  edited by Brian Henry
Robert Hayden
  edited by Laurence Goldstein and Robert Chrisman
Charles Simic
  edited by Bruce Weigl
On Gwendolyn Brooks
  edited by Stephen Caldwell Wright
On William Stafford
  edited by Tom Andrews
Denise Levertov
  edited with an introduction by Albert Gelpi
The Poetry of W. D. Snodgrass
  edited by Stephen Haven
On the Poetry of Philip Levine
  edited by Christopher Buckley
James Wright
  edited by Peter Stitt and Frank Graziano
Anne Sexton
  edited by Steven E. Colburn
On the Poetry of Galway Kinnell
  edited by Howard Nelson
Robert Creeley's Life and Work
  edited by John Wilson
On the Poetry of Allen Ginsberg
  edited by Lewis Hyde
Reading Adrienne Rich
  edited by Jane Roberta Cooper
Elizabeth Bishop and Her Art
  edited by Lloyd Schwartz and Sybil P. Estess